THE LOVE FIGHT

ACHIEVERS WANT SUCCESS

How ACHIEVERS & CONNECTORS
Can Build a Marriage that Lasts

CONNECTORS WANT RELATIONSHIPS

FLORIDA
HOSPITAL
Since 1908

THE LOVE FIGHT

TONY FERRETTI, PhD & PETER J. WEISS, MD

FLORIDA
HOSPITAL

EDITOR-IN-CHIEF	Todd Chobotar
MANAGING EDITOR	David Biebel, DMin
PEER REVIEWERS	Ted Hamilton, MD, Stephanie Lind, MBA
	Herdley Paolini, PhD, Karen Tilstra, PhD
	Aliza Rosen, MD, Terri Schultz, PhD
PRODUCTION	Lillian Boyd
COPY EDITOR	Pam Nordberg
PHOTOGRAPHY	Spencer Freeman
COVER DESIGN	Dual Identity
INTERIOR DESIGN	Kathy Curtis

For volume discounts please contact special sales at:
HealthProducts@FLHosp.org | 407-303-1929

Library of Congress Control number: 2014954208

Printed in the United States of America.
PR 14 13 12 11 10 9 8 7 6 5 4 3 2 1
ISBN 13: 978-0-9904191-2-9

For other life changing resources visit:
FloridaHospitalPublishing.com
CreationHealth.com

Contents

To our wives, with gratitude for helping us become the husbands and fathers we wish to be.

Introduction

THE LOVE FIGHT AND POWER FAILURES

You're mystified. You've seen this drama repeated over and over again, and you just can't understand how it happens. A public figure—perhaps a powerful businessman, community leader, star athlete, or a leading politician—destroys his marriage and family life through an extramarital affair. You're left shaking your head and thinking, "He had it all. What happened? How could he throw it all away?" It's simple; he lost the Love Fight.

This is so common that it's not even shocking anymore. More than 40 percent of first marriages end in divorce.[1, 2] Many powerful men and women are currently living or preparing to live out this tale of heartbreak. As we said, you've seen it. We've seen it too. Dr. Ferretti sees this story or something very similar in his counseling practice literally every workday. Dr. Weiss sees this in healthcare and in the world of business. We like to call these breakups the "Power Failure Syndrome"—powerful people, who seemingly have it all, ultimately fail in their relationships with spouses, families, and friends. Power Failures are the result of losing the Love Fight, and they happen frequently.

If you're in a relationship, you're in the Love Fight too. Every marriage involves conflicts, large and small. Our use of the term "Love Fight" encompasses all of the natural disagreements and conflicts inherent in intimate relationships. "Winning" the Love Fight means coming together in a happy, committed relationship. It requires focusing on the marriage, not winning the actual disagreement at the moment. In losing the Love Fight, relationships are destroyed.

Back to our power player—slowly, over the next several months, his family's story trickles out. The wife has given a few interviews. Friends of the older children have spoken off the record to journalists. Even old girlfriends from college or graduate school have turned up on daytime cable television. Collectively, they paint a picture of a man who is intelligent, successful, and often charming to new acquaintances, but who is also highly competitive, driven to succeed, controlling, and emotionally distant from his family and friends.

So it's a little more understandable now. He wasn't a perfect person, and he didn't really have it all in the first place. Sure, he was successful in business or politics, but his family life was never what it could have been. His wife and children were not his first priority. His marriage and family ranked a distant second to the pursuit of power and possessions.

After the breakup, then what? His next stop may be to a marriage counselor or psychologist, someone like Dr. Ferretti—or maybe not. Some men will repeat the same behavior rather than changing. What are two or three divorces for a captain of industry? One divorce practically comes with the territory. However, the family may or may not recover, and a lot of emotional, financial, and spiritual damage has already been done.

The rising divorce rates for second and third marriages, estimated at 60–67 percent and 70–73 percent, respectively, suggest that many do not learn from experience.[2] How many of these folks have you heard say, "I just haven't found the right person?"

A successful marriage is not all about finding the "right person" and living happily ever after. In committed relationships there are always going to be conflicts or fights. The question is will you fight *for* the relationship or *against* each other? Successful couples win the Love Fight together by finding themselves, clarifying their values, and making changes to strengthen the relationship. Unfortunately, justifying your own behavior and blaming your spouse is typically easier than changing your approach to relationships.

ACHIEVERS AND CONNECTORS

The Love Fight and Power Failure Syndrome aren't limited to wealthy and powerful men, though they represent the stereotype with which most people are familiar. Power Failures can occur at all levels of society and not just with men; in today's world of gender equality, women often play the leading role.

Essentially this syndrome is about individuals with a certain personality type—the driven high achiever—and how their often-harmful habits and misplaced priorities can destroy the very relationships they say they want. In this book, we'll call them "Achievers." It really doesn't matter if this person is a man or a woman. The relationship issues and interpersonal dynamics flow from the personality features, not the gender.

Although any individual Achiever may marry a spouse of any personality, in our experience Achievers often marry individuals who are more focused on relationships—perhaps, consciously or subconsciously, making up for their deficiencies in this area. In this book we call these relationship-focused individuals "Connectors." We feel it is this type of Achiever/Connector marriage that is at high risk for a Power Failure, and it's this pattern we're addressing in this book. We call it the "A/C Marriage."

Stereotypically, men are often seen as Achievers and women as Connectors, and like many stereotypes there is some validity to it. Our experience and public media reporting leads us to believe that the male/female ratio for the Achiever in A/C marriages is well over 50/50, perhaps 70/30 or more. However, we see that male/female ratio changing as leadership roles in the workplace become more even between men and women. Depending on your social circle, you will probably be able to call to mind instances of each gender representing the Achiever and the Connector. In this book, we use examples of both men and women who exhibit the characteristics we're addressing.

Regardless of who is the Achiever or Connector, a Power Failure affects all family members in a very destructive manner. Having devoted his career to healing marriages, Dr. Ferretti knows how difficult it is to help *after* the power fails. Often the damage to the family can't be repaired and he's limited to helping people move on with their lives after the home is torn apart. We wrote this book to alert you to the underlying causes of the Power Failure Syndrome and to give you tools and strategies to prevent it and provide ways to heal your relationship. We want you to win the Love Fight to have a happy and healthy family life.

WHO ARE WE?

Dr. Ferretti has spent more than twenty years as a practicing psychologist helping others to step off the destructive path leading to broken relationships. The Power Failure Syndrome happens because the same traits that propel people to the top in business cause turmoil in their personal lives. Dr. Ferretti has helped numerous high achievers recognize the addictive nature of power, control, and success and the importance of maintaining healthy relationships. In his work with professionals and couples, he helps them to understand the Love Fight and to identify the unhealthy thoughts, actions, and interactions that cause relationship problems and lead to potentially destructive behaviors.

On a personal note, Dr. Ferretti himself is a naturally hard-working, driven, and competitive person, which has enabled him to have a deep understanding of his clients and the Power Failure Syndrome. But fortunately, he's been able to follow his own advice, and he's done the work to change and achieve an appropriate balance of career, marriage, family, and friends in his life. He continues to develop a greater appreciation for relationships, emotional connectedness, and defining success through significance in relationships over personal achievements.

Dr. Weiss has also seen this pattern of success-at-work/divorce-at-home repeatedly. As a practicing physician and as a health care administrator, he has been surrounded by high-achieving professionals and has had a close-up view of the damaging effects of power and control.

He has counseled staff on personality conflicts and has been personally affected by unbridled competition for the corporate top spots.

For a time, Dr. Weiss the Achiever was caught up in the "work is life" mentality but began to question his own values and broke free to live differently.

WHY WE'RE WRITING

Our primary purpose is to help you, the Achiever, in your relationships, by passing along what we've learned. Most people have to learn these lessons the hard way, but you can profit from our experience. We are writing directly to you, the Achiever, because we know it's very hard for you to acknowledge problems and seek help. But, in fact, more than two-thirds of those who have divorced would advise others to work it out or see a counselor.[3]

Frankly, change is difficult for almost everyone, but particularly for alpha types who like to be in charge, making things happen. Of course, this book won't solve all of your relationship problems. Our goal is simply to help you see things differently, and in so doing make it easier for you to change. We also want to help you identify what needs to change and how to go about making change happen.

Perhaps you're not the driven, overachieving type, but you may recognize your spouse in these pages. You might be a Connector. This book is for you, too. It's not for flinging at your mate, but rather to help you understand him or her, yourself, and your relationship a little bit better. Maybe you have never considered your role in any marital issues. It takes two to make a marriage, but, as we hope to make clear, relationships work best when all parties are focused on understanding and improving themselves. You, too, can begin to see things differently and to change yourself, which will improve your relationships.

Some Achievers are married to other Achievers. Long common in Hollywood, marriages between highly successful and powerful individuals are increasingly common in the professional and business worlds. If this is you, understand that your relationship is at special risk.

When couples are in danger of losing the Love Fight, it's typically the Connector spouse who is able to seek help and convince his or her mate to enter couples therapy. Achievers are often quite resistant. When two Achievers are married to each other, the likelihood of working out relationship problems goes down significantly, unless one becomes willing to make the first move. Achiever or Connector, whichever you may be, why not make that first move yourself?

Thankfully, many couples are not yet in a Power Failure situation. But what about "low power" relationships? We think these are even more common. How many marriages are truly working as well as possible? Low power marriages, where partners remain together as roommates with little emotional connection or intimacy, can be caused by the same behaviors but at a lesser intensity than we see in Power Failure situations. In such relationships, children may learn to avoid conflict, to hide their

> We've distilled our most critical relationship wisdom into short "attitudes and actions," which are highlighted in boxes like this.

feelings, not to expect intimacy in their own relationships, and that marriage simply isn't that great. Is that what you'd like your children to take away from your marriage example? After all, being married can be one of the best things in life. Research has shown that married people are on average happier, healthier, and wealthier than similar but unmarried individuals. The power doesn't have to fail. Warning signs are usually present well in advance of a Power Failure. We'd like to help you understand the Love Fight, recognize the danger signs, and act on them early.

In this book, we hope to help you learn what we've learned:

- You can have a fulfilling marriage.
- You can achieve greater balance in your life.
- You can be more connected to others.
- It all starts with changing yourself.

We invite you to complete the self-assessments found throughout the book. The self-assessment questions are intended to help you to evaluate your own life and relationships. Invest some time to reflect on the issues raised. And for those who just want the bottom line, we've further compressed our message to the bare essentials at the close of each chapter.

We hope these words will help you power up your existing relationships to find the joy and happiness that comes from putting people ahead of possessions. We want you to be as successful at home as you are at work.

The Love Fight

Is It a Love Worth Fighting For?

JESSICA'S STORY

Jessica sat quietly crying again at the kitchen counter. She had managed to get showered and dressed without breaking down, but there was no holding back the tears now that she was alone at breakfast. It had been three days since her husband, Michael, had moved out.

As Jessica thought back about the recent upheaval in her life, she was obviously sad but also perplexed. *How did it come to this?* she wondered. She had been so happy when she and Michael had begun dating shortly after they met twenty-two years ago. Michael had just graduated from medical school—a young, handsome, and confident surgical intern.

Jessica was several years out of college with a BS degree in exercise physiology and working as a yoga and fitness instructor at the university's wellness center. At that time in her life, Jessica was looking for a partner who could provide security and stability, unlike what she'd seen in her parents' relationship. When her father had left her mother—that was that—her mother had no husband and no income. Jessica had always worried that she might experience the same fate.

She was looking for someone different from her father, someone better. Jessica recognized Michael's talent and was attracted by his confident, self-assured manner in the hospital. Michael was her rock, and she thought he would always be there for her. Michael wasn't perfect; that wasn't the point. At times he could be like the absent-minded professor—extremely intelligent and a great doctor but awkward in social situations and with very little street smarts outside of work.

He seemed to need help with the ordinary, mundane tasks of life and had no close friends. Jessica figured she and Michael were a perfect fit. She had the skills to run a household and raise children, and she was their social connector. She thought surely she could teach Michael some social skills. Although occasionally embarrassing, his ineptness endeared her to him all the more. The attraction was mutual, and very soon they were an item.

I remember feeling that I was just "settling" for less than I wanted.

It had all seemed so simple then. They were both young, in their mid-twenties, and in love. Of course, Michael worked hard and Jessica understood that. She recognized the demands of a surgical practice, but Michael did seem interested in her when they were together. Occasionally he was short with her, but she chalked that up to the stress he was under at work, and Jessica assumed that Michael would loosen up in time. She also assumed they would be seeing much more of each other once they were married and Michael had graduated from residency. All in all she anticipated a happy life with him. They were engaged at the end of his internship and married a year later.

Jessica continued to work at the wellness center, but it was hard to work full time and keep the home running, too. Michael was working so hard—sixty to seventy hours a week in those days—that they didn't have much time together. Once pregnant with their first child, she decided to cut her work schedule back to fifteen hours per week. During her maternity leave she briefly considered quitting all together, but then realized how much she missed the daily interactions with friends and clients at the center. So after six weeks off, she returned to a twenty-hour-per-week schedule. Looking back at that time, it had seemed to Jessica that hers was the ideal life.

Boy, she thought, *life sure got more complicated after that.* With two young children by the time Michael graduated from residency, and still working at the wellness center, she had her hands full. She had mistakenly assumed that they would have more time together after he completed his surgical training; instead, it seemed like life just got even busier. They moved to a smaller city where Michael began his surgical career, and as Michael said, "You don't build a career by taking time off."

Although he was in business for himself, he was at the hospital just as much as when he was a resident. Jessica didn't really understand it, but Michael was insistent on working. "This is what it takes to be a good surgeon. It doesn't help to complain about it," he would say. *Was I a complainer and a nag?* Jessica wondered. *I didn't want to be. After all, I lived in a beautiful house on the water, owned a brand new car, and his income meant I didn't have to work.*

At the time, it seemed like a nice life - plenty of money, a nice house, a fulfilling job, good friends, and status in the community.

Although she didn't have to work, Jessica decided to take a part-time position at a boutique women's-only fitness center after connecting with the owner, Amy, at a 5k race sponsored by the center. Soon she was working twenty hours a week again as a yoga instructor, running coach, and race organizer. *I enjoyed that time with the kids and my work at the wellness center,* she thought, *but I still missed my husband. Michael just wasn't around much back then. How was I supposed to spend my time? I raised the kids and managed the home. But did he appreciate me? If he did, he sure didn't share it.*

Just as quickly, Michael became an important figure in town. He and Jessica began mixing in a high-income social circle. It was a new experience for both of them to be asked to cocktail parties and invited to join a country club. Although Jessica didn't know many members, Michael insisted on joining. "It's good for my career, and it's important for you to be there with me," he said. Jessica did meet many other physicians' wives and developed an increasing circle of friends. Her best friend was Susan, whose husband was a prominent cardiologist. Like Jessica, Susan enjoyed exercise. A competitive triathlete, Susan lived down the street and had children slightly older than Jessica's sons, Bill and Jeff. Susan and Jessica became frequent running partners and confidants. At the time, it seemed like a nice life—plenty of money, a nice house, a fulfilling job, good friends, and status in the community.

Now I'm not so sure. Was that what I wanted? Was that what I said "I do" for? Jessica wondered. *What do I want now? I thought he'd be home more. I had everything but Michael. I thought he'd be a great dad and husband. I guess I hoped he would change, but it hasn't happened. Where did all the years go?*

The time when the children were in elementary, junior high, and high school seemed like a blur. Life was in constant motion in those days. As the children became more independent teenagers, she increased her hours at the fitness center. Four years ago, when Amy had put the center up for sale, Jessica jumped at the chance to buy it. "How can I let it go to someone else?" she asked Susan. "I love it there. It's practically my second home." When Susan offered to help staff the center, Jessica knew she wanted to make it happen. Michael was cool to the idea but eventually agreed to the purchase. Since then, Jessica had managed to do it all. She ran the center, maintained the home, and still stayed involved with the boys' activities; Bill played soccer and Jeff was active in academic clubs and competitions.

She and Michael had very little time together, but she still enjoyed it when they did. *Did I really enjoy our time together, or was I lying to myself?* she wondered. *I remember feeling that I was just "settling" for less than I wanted. I sensed we were growing apart and that Michael wasn't changing.*

How come I didn't do anything about it? Why didn't I speak up and insist on counseling? Our relationship got only the scraps. I don't think it was ever a high priority for Michael.

Now that Bill, age twenty, and Jeff, eighteen, were off to college, Jessica had a less hectic life. But now she reflected back on just how busy she had been with her own activities and how little time she and Michael really had spent with each other. *Perhaps I was ignoring Michael with my focus on the center and the boys. Maybe I could have given our relationship more time. But he certainly didn't give me much time. It seems like he only paid attention to me when he wanted sex. What was I supposed to do? At the center, at least I had friends.*

Looking back, Jessica recalled that she had tried to talk with Michael about their growing disconnection several times through the years, but he always had become angry and pointed out all the things he had provided through his hard work. But it seemed that he never wanted to talk about their relationship, or about her needs and her feelings. *I guess I shouldn't be surprised, she mused. He never has talked about those issues. But now this! How could he? He couldn't find the time for me, but he sure found time for her.*

He also had about as much emotional sensitivity as a rock.

Jessica had heard of the affair through her network of friends at the fitness center. Even Susan knew. At first, she didn't believe it. *I didn't want to believe it. I still don't want to believe it, but it's true. It's all true,* she said to herself.

After creating a wonderful family, beautiful home, and social network of friends together, Jessica was having a hard time understanding how Michael could be with someone else. She stopped crying and suddenly became angry. *He's been carrying on with her for three years. And there were others before this one. How many nurses has he been with when he should have been with me? He's been out there sleeping around and he won't even talk with me.*

When she had confronted Michael, he hadn't even tried to deny the affair. He had just walked out. She had followed him angrily, asking for some explanation, but he had told her flatly that there was nothing to discuss. Later that day he had returned for some clothes and personal items and said he was sorry and needed to think things over. He didn't have much more to say, and Jessica was so angry she could hardly think straight, so she wouldn't have been able to carry on a conversation then, even if he had wanted to talk.

That was three days ago, and Jessica was now more sad than angry. She had spoken to Michael by telephone the previous night and had asked him to come home. As usual, Michael had an overly full patient schedule but said that he would be home tonight after the workday. *So he's coming home tonight. Now what?* she wondered. *How do I act around him? What do I say? Where are we headed? How did it come to this? Do I throw it all away and tell him to start packing, or do we try to work it out? What's he thinking? Has he already made his decision?*

MICHAEL'S STORY

Michael was at the hospital. He had a full surgical schedule and wasn't going to cancel any cases because of personal issues. That was not his way. He'd rather just avoid thinking about it, and of course, this same avoidant behavior had been a major factor in the devolution of his relationship with Jessica. Michael had always run from emotional issues, perhaps not realizing that in doing so he was also running from his wife.

Living out of a hotel room had been inconvenient, but he was determined to go back home tonight even though he hadn't given too much thought to the future of his marriage over the past three days, suppressing the issue by focusing on work. He'd been thinking, *A good doctor cares for his patients first. Sure, I've got a family "situation," but who doesn't?*

Michael had seen this particular situation coming for years. He had grown tired of Jessica's seemingly constant nagging about his busy practice and on-call schedule. She also spent much of her time and energy at the fitness center and with the boys, and she didn't focus on his needs. She never seemed excited about sex or about him anymore. He knew that his marriage wasn't working, and he knew why. *She doesn't appreciate me for who I am, like she used to. I am who I am—a doctor, a good doctor—and I work hard, he reckoned. My patients value me, my staff respects me, and now I've found another woman who appreciates me, too. Why doesn't my wife admire me and attend to me like they do?*

This was the truth. At this point in their relationship, Jessica really didn't appreciate Michael for who he was anymore. Frankly, Michael was demanding, arrogant, and out of touch with his own emotions. Often insensitive, he had become much more so over time. The newfound power and wealth from his surgical practice had magnified his self-centeredness and entitlement mentality. He never really thought too much about Jessica. She was just always there to take care of him. His needs always came first, and achieving material success and status in the community was pretty much all he seemed to care about.

Even though they had been married twenty-one years, Michael had not achieved true emotional intimacy with Jessica. In fact, he had never been emotionally connected to anyone, and Jessica's emotional demands wore on him. Often described by others as "wound tight," being relaxed and vulnerable was not his nature. In fact, Michael found it was just easier to be at work where he was in his element. He enjoyed being in control and being important to the patients and hospital staff. In this environment Michael also found many admiring nurses—women who looked up to him, like Jessica used to do when they began dating.

Well, Michael thought, *now it's out in the open.* He had known it would be someday. He'd been having affairs for the previous five years of his marriage. Michael wasn't surprised at Jessica's reaction, and his conscience was bothering him. *Why do I feel so guilty? She's been ignoring me for years. I've been a good provider and she should have appreciated that,* he thought. *I deserve to have someone who cares for me. I want a wife who respects me.*

Although he had told her he would be home this evening

> While the common phrase is "opposites attract," many opposites have a difficult time sustaining their original magnetism.

after work, he wasn't so self-assured about how to handle this situation. *Now what? How do I act around her? What do I say? Where are we headed? How did it come to this?*

How Did It Come to This?

How *did* it come to this? In marriage counseling, couples ask this question all the time. Effective counselors help them work out the answer for themselves. But since you are only observers in Jessica and Michael's crisis, we'll go ahead and tell you how and why this happened.

First, realize that Jessica and Michael were really in love and committed to each other when they wed. Neither went to the altar thinking that it might not work out or that each wasn't fully committed to the other. But somewhere along the way they got off track. Let's begin by looking at some of their basic personality traits and expectations for their marriage.

Michael, although intelligent and accomplished, has never been there emotionally for Jessica. He didn't intentionally ignore her feelings; he hasn't been capable of responding to them. He simply doesn't understand emotions. He is typically not aware of the emotional state of others or even himself, and never learned to be a sensitive or nurturing person. As a provider, Michael seemed to be the rock Jessica was looking for, a secure and stable breadwinner with great potential. Unfortunately, he also had about as much emotional sensitivity as a rock.

Michael is also much more introverted and analytical than Jessica. Although he can force a socially adequate response when he meets new people, he has a hard time maintaining it and making deep connections. With little perception of others' boundaries and feelings, he can be socially inept. In conversation, for example, he doesn't realize when others are bored or uncomfortable and want to change the subject away from his tales of surgery.

He tends to trust only himself and thus avoids working through conflicts with others. In any disagreement, he will steadfastly adhere to his own position on the matter in dispute. The one emotion he does express is anger, usually when he's being challenged. Being angry is easier for him than admitting he might be wrong.

On the other hand, Jessica is a people pleaser and caretaker. She expresses love for others through service, which, combined with her interest in fitness, led her into her career. Jessica experiences love from others through their attention to her, especially verbal expressions of love or praise and simply spending time together. She is an outgoing, emotional, and social person who loves being with people. Social status, wealth, and material possessions are not unimportant to her, but being connected to family and friends is most important. However, like many people, Jessica is also highly concerned with appearances and is not comfortable confronting others or admitting to problems in her life. Above all else, she hates to have others be unhappy with her, fearing disapproval or rejection.

Michael's expectations for the relationship were simply that Jessica would be there to take care of his needs and that he would be making a living. He hadn't really given any thought to what else she might need. Jessica expected Michael to be a good provider, but she also expected that he would grow into a more warm and open person and that he would be spending a lot more time with her once out of training.

Initially, Michael and Jessica were both living the "knight in shining armor rescues the damsel in distress" fantasy. Jessica was looking for a solid provider, and Michael could rescue her by virtue of his economic prowess.

Michael was looking for someone to take care of him, and that was right up Jessica's alley. Both Jessica and Michael had voids and deficits in their lives that each of them was attempting to fill through the other. So they were forming a codependent relationship right from the start. Codependency

> Frustrations can be minor, but if they go unresolved long enough, anger and resentment always follow.

happens when one partner takes responsibility for the other person, which prevents the other person from taking responsibility for himself or herself. Unfortunately, although seeming like an ideal partnering, this "filling the other's void" can become detrimental with time, inhibiting partners from learning and growing into a deeper relationship.

None of Michael or Jessica's personality traits are unusual or abnormal. In fact, they are quite common. That's why we're writing to you. We'll talk about how they developed these traits later, but for now just understand this is how they were when they fell in love and got married.

At first, life together was great. Their mix of personality traits was seemingly complementary. Jessica enjoyed caring for Michael and the heightened social status that came with dating a doctor. She was always doing little things for him—for example, planning surprise picnic dinners after a night on call, picking his white coats up from the cleaners, and getting his car washed and waxed. Michael welcomed the attention that he received from Jessica early in their relationship and he reciprocated. He bought Jessica gifts and took her to nice restaurants. They were both happy and anxiously looked forward to getting married.

Because of her personality, Jessica coordinated all of the social events and maintained the friendships that they made. She was much better at nurturing relationships and getting close to people. Her caretaking behavior together with Michael's lack of emotional awareness led to Jessica shouldering the emotional demands for both of them. For example, when Michael's mother became seriously ill during their courtship, Jessica was more emotionally affected and provided more support to Michael's parents than Michael himself did. Jessica didn't think too much about it at the time, but essentially she was helping Michael avoid legitimate emotions that he was unwilling to face. Michael was able to avoid dealing with uncomfortable feelings and taking responsibility for comforting his mother. This unhealthy pattern of behavior continued in different forms over the years of their marriage.

This is often how the Love Fight develops in A/C relationships. While the common phrase is "opposites attract," many opposites have a difficult time sustaining their original magnetism. In fact, for many pairs of opposites, what initially attracts each to their partner can become the very same trait that becomes annoying years later. In a healthy relationship, the partners flex and work to temper or accommodate their differences and win the fight. Unfortunately, in many struggling marriages, the differences are magnified over time and the partners grow further apart, risking a Power Failure. In the case of Jessica and Michael, her nurturing and social nature led her to be consumed with her children, her work at the fitness center, and her friends. Michael's responsible and hard-working nature resulted in long hours at the hospital and neglecting his family.

In addition, Jessica's need for attention and love eventually became irritating to Michael. Wasn't he providing a nice house, cars, money, and status? In turn, his emotional aloofness became increasingly frustrating and annoying to Jessica over time. Jessica felt like a nagging mother, and Michael felt as if he was being treated like a petulant child. Slowly, over the months and years, things began to change. Life got more complicated when they married, purchased a house, started a family. Suddenly, there was a lot more responsibility resting on both of their shoulders. Jessica took on the increasing load of managing the household while Michael continued to throw himself into his work. Predictably, they made less and less time for each other.

Little things happened that began to create a web of frustration, anger, and resentment in their relationship. For example:

> One morning their youngest child, Jeff, only eight at the time, hit a curb with the front tire of his bike and was thrown onto the sidewalk. A neighbor called 911 and Jeff was rushed to the ER. He required seventeen stitches to close his head laceration and was admitted overnight for observation due to his concussion and vomiting. Michael was at his office with patients when Jessica called from the hospital. He sized up the clinical situation quickly in his own mind: Jeff sounds okay. There doesn't seem to be anything for me to do there, but I've got a lot going on here. We don't both need to be at the hospital. Jessica's got it covered. He told Jessica he would see her after the office closed. He also asked Jessica to telephone with an update when the doctors checked on Jeff in the afternoon. Jessica was furious! She thought, How can he be so cold and uncaring? Actually, it never even occurred to Michael that both Jessica and Jeff might need emotional support from him. He considered only the medical issues at hand and was satisfied with that situation. Therefore, he felt that no action on his part was needed. Of course, Jessica was beside herself with anger and didn't speak to him for several days.

And another example:

> After a long day at the hospital, Michael was paying the bills and flipped out when he opened Jessica's monthly credit card bill to discover over $2,500 in charges for a value-priced road bike that she bought for herself in addition to some electronics for the boys. Jessica had never thought too much about spending money. Even though the fitness

center provided almost no income, from Jessica's point of view, they had plenty of cash and she was working hard too. She also frequently bought high-priced gifts for her family and friends. Michael was livid when he saw the charges and verbally unloaded on Jessica. *"You don't respect me! You don't appreciate how hard I work to earn that money. We don't need those things anyway. What's the matter with you?"* he yelled. In his fit of anger, he dumped out her purse and cut up all of her cards. For the next two months, he closely monitored the online bank statements. Eventually he relented and allowed Jessica to obtain replacement cards. But Michael would continue to rehash this issue long into the future as a means of justifying his overreaction.

Although these may sound like extreme episodes to some, they represent typical emotional flash points of marriage. Different expectations lead to frustration and anger. Jessica expected Michael to be there emotionally for her in a time of crisis. Michael expected Jessica to spend less and save more. In an ideal world, Michael and Jessica would have talked through these differences and come to a compromise. But this can be hard. In Michael's and Jessica's case, they seemingly couldn't and didn't. So they became increasingly frustrated with each other. Frustrations can be minor, but if they go unresolved long enough, anger and resentment always follow.

When a couple doesn't resolve conflict through discussion, mutual understanding, and agreement, there are often two simplistic coping mechanisms—shutting down or lashing out. Michael and Jessica both chose to shut down to each other. Their frustration turned to anger, and the chronic anger turned to resentment, which is "anger with a history."

Over the years, the resentments between Jessica and Michael built up slowly but relentlessly. Resentment is a powerful enemy of emotional connection. There is no way to be closer when you're harboring resentments about your partner, except by releasing these negative feelings. Unfortunately for their relationship, both Michael and Jessica are stubborn and strong willed. Since neither was willing or prepared to release their resentments, they coped by gradually distancing themselves through emotional detachment followed by behavioral detachment.

Jessica began to focus more on raising the boys, her role at the fitness center, and other more social activities. Michael's detaching behavior was to work even more, with more time spent at the office and hospital, less time for his wife and children. And he became more open to being taken care of by a woman other than his wife.

The final step along this path of increasing resentment is self-destruction. In Michael's case, it happened through his extramarital affair; in others,

How Are Your Relationships?
It's common to be "successful" in business but to fail in personal relationships— to be possessions- rich/ relationships-poor. Many high achievers find themselves here. People matter more than things. Attend to the people in your life.

it may be expressed as excessive spending, overuse of alcohol or drugs, addiction to pornography, compulsive overeating, or some other form of escape. The point is that if the frustration and anger are not addressed and resolved, they often lead to destructive behaviors. Michael and Jessica refused to face their relationship problems until they reached this critical stage.

When emotional detachment is expressed through relationship-destructive behavior, a Power Failure is looming. Such behaviors always threaten a marriage. And everything tends to get worse with the passing of time until there is either an accommodation, such as an enduring but loveless marriage "for the sake of the kids," or alternatively, a crisis. Michael and Jessica are facing their crisis now.

COULD THIS HAPPEN TO YOU?

So, could this happen to you? Let's distill Michael and Jessica's story down to the essentials before you answer. Michael and Jessica were in love but had different personalities and expectations for their married life. When each did not meet the expectations of the other, conflicts occurred and they were not able to, or chose not to, talk through their disagreements to amicably resolve them. Instead, the frustration built into anger and the anger into resentment. Resentment led to detachment in thought and behavior.

In our view, the single most important underlying cause of the chronic deterioration in their relationship was their inability to manage the Love Fight. By lashing out or shutting down and avoiding responsibility for their own issues, they both contributed to the current crisis.

Baseline characteristics of their relationship:

- Different personalities
- Different expectations
- Unable or unwilling to talk through conflict to resolution

With time:

- Conflicts grew
- Frustration built
- Chronic anger developed
- Resentments formed and intensified
- Detachment in thought developed
- Detachment in behavior developed
- CRISIS!

Back to the question, could it happen to you? Of course it could happen to you. It could happen to any of us. Both authors are high-performing professionals. And we have both been over the top in drive and ambition. We are also both married and have children. Fortunately, we haven't had Power Failures, but we've been underpowered in our relationships. Everything that we're writing about we have also learned through personal and/or clinical experience.

Here are a couple of experiences that we're not proud of but illustrate the issues:

Dr. Ferretti: Early in our marriage, my wife suffered a miscarriage at seven weeks of pregnancy. Naturally, Allison was devastated and it didn't help that she needed a surgical procedure afterward to ensure her own health. I obviously wasn't connecting to her feelings when I began to suggest that we schedule this procedure around my busy office practice. Fortunately, the obstetrician called me out on this with a direct confrontation about Allison's need for emotional support and my own self-important priorities. I got the message and took care of Allison first. She was my number-one priority, and the doctor helped me to see that. I wound up writing him a thank-you letter when I fully appreciated how he had helped me focus on my wife before my practice.

> **Cultivate Your Relationships**
> So many people, when faced with difficulty in their own relationships, begin to look elsewhere and think, *The grass is greener on the other side of the fence. There are others who would be better for me than my spouse.* Sometimes the grass is greener on the other side, because your neighbor keeps it watered. Are you watering your own grass? Can you "green up" your own lawn? Water your own grass before you look over the fence at your neighbor's lawn.

Dr. Weiss: My wife, Sharon, suffered an attack of abdominal pain at work that was so severe she needed me to pick her up and take her to the doctor. She gradually felt better at the doctor's office, but he wanted to do some lab tests and imaging procedures that would take two hours or so. Oblivious to Sharon's feelings, I went back to the office while she had the studies and returned when they were finished. She just couldn't understand why I had abandoned her, and I couldn't understand (until many years later) why she felt abandoned.

We don't believe that we were unusually insensitive people when we married our respective spouses. Men like us are pretty common in American life today. If you read a newspaper or watch TV, you've seen them. It's a big group spread across many fields of endeavor, including business, law, politics, athletics, and medicine. You might even be one yourself, or perhaps you're married to one. That's why we wrote this book.

We think Power Failures can happen to anyone, especially in today's society, which can undermine the creation and sustenance of deep relationships, even in marriage. Our purpose is to prevent Power Failures by helping you power up your marriage and relationships. Let's start by understanding what it takes to create a strong married relationship and then examine in more detail some of the societal and personality issues that may be harming your relationships.

THE BOTTOM LINE:

- A fulfilling marriage takes *work*—work from *both* partners. So if you're not part of the solution, you are part of the problem.
- Life gets complicated and stressful quickly. The events of life *will* affect your marriage.
- *Pay attention* to your relationships. Warning signs always come before a crisis. Recognize them and take action early.

Success
or failure in marriage
is determined
by both partners.

They Don't Understand Me!

Achievers and Connectors in Relationships

In our story, Michael and Jessica represent composites drawn from Dr. Ferretti's experience with many couples, designed to illustrate a common pattern—the Power Failure Syndrome in the Achiever/Connector marriage. Although they are fictional characters, they illustrate issues that are very real for many Achiever/Connector couples.

ACHIEVING AND CONNECTING

This chapter focuses on the personality characteristics or behavioral traits we have labeled "achieving" and "connecting." When we use "achieving" and "connecting" or related terms with a lower case "a" or "c," we use them as they are commonly understood in ordinary parlance. When we use "Achiever" or "Connector" with capital letters, we mean a certain personality type that we have identified and named, based on our experience, which is not related to any formal scientific research or other systems of cataloging personality.

Both achieving and connecting are valuable but distinct aspects of most individuals' personalities. Achieving can be expressed as the desire to get things accomplished, while connecting is the desire to be in community with others. Although we do not view them as complete opposites, we believe they are often conflicting, and we think that few individuals possess both characteristics to a high degree. For discussion purposes, you can envision them at opposite ends of a continuum.

Like other personality traits, sometimes the achieving or connecting trait can be so strong as to be in some ways counterproductive to the individual. The central theme of this book is that the achievement drive is so strong in some individuals that, while they may become very successful in their careers, this same drive coupled with less connecting drive causes failure in their interpersonal relationships. These individuals are capital A Achievers. In lower case letters they might be termed overachievers. Connectors, on the other hand, are more motivated by the desire to be in relationship with others. They have an internal drive to be part of a family, a church, or other formal or informal community. Friends and personal relationships are very important to them. Of course, Connectors build careers and achieve things as well, but their success doesn't come at the expense of their relationships.

> Both achieving and connecting are valuable but distinct aspects of most individuals' personalities.

ACHIEVERS

An Achiever is a person whose identity is built around accomplishments. Their personal sense of value comes from their accomplishments—often with an implied "what have you done for me lately?" They may feel a relentless internal pressure to produce and aren't able to gain self-worth from other sources or activities.

A high drive to achieve has obvious value. A strong work ethic, high productivity, and top performance lead to success in many arenas. Achievers work very hard to get ahead in life and apply themselves fully to accomplish great things. Goal-oriented, driven, and perseverant through challenging times, Achievers often view demanding tasks as opportunities for growth. Achievers are the people you want at your company. They take initiative, are committed to a project from start to finish, and are open to learning as a means of improving. Achievers' motivation and drive are powerful traits that can serve them well in many aspects of their lives.

But Achievers can have a difficult time turning off their intensity, drive, and determination. Setting high (even unrealistic) standards for themselves and others, Achievers can be all-or-nothing individuals unable to approach many issues with moderation. Typically they are usually thinking about work or other items on their to-do list. Relaxing or taking some time off may be very hard for an Achiever unless some major success has been achieved and nothing else is pressing. Some Achievers are also perfectionists, which further complicates their already intense approach to life.

Achievers get satisfaction from accomplishments—the bigger the better. They relish challenges and have a strong orientation toward problem solving, but often lack interpersonal skills. Achievers may prefer to "Do it myself to make sure it's done right." Avoiding delegation and difficult conversations, they often expect others to fall in behind or get out of the way as they march down the path of production. Although Achievers may make a great deal of money, achievement is the primary motivator, and the money either comes along with success or represents a way of keeping score of what's been accomplished.

In general, Achievers like to be their own boss, in charge of their own destiny, while striving to maintain an image of competence and control. They are self-reliant, independent, competitive, and self-critical. Achievers also tend to be analytical, logical, and rational in their approach to problems and conflict. Unfortunately, some of these characteristics are not conducive to relationships, which require cooperation, compromise, and empathy.

Michael is an Achiever. He wanted to be a doctor since he was a child and was determined to make it happen. Naturally, he focused on making good grades, excelling in sports, and volunteering to build a broader résumé and get into the "best" college. In college, Michael studied compulsively to get into the "best" medical school. In medical school he worked hard to get selected for the "best" residency. As a resident, he focused on performing in order to have his pick of private practice jobs. By the time he met Jessica, he was well on his way toward being a great surgeon and getting that plum job. When he finally "arrived" in private practice, he loved it. He was his own boss, achieving through surgery and receiving regular positive feedback in the form of income as well as compliments from patients and the hospital staff.

Here are some of the potentially helpful and unhelpful characteristics of Achievers:

| CHARACTERISTICS OF ACHIEVERS ||
HELPFUL	UNHELPFUL
Hardworking	Obsessed with getting job done
Willing to be a leader	Incapable of following
Confident	Arrogant
Competitive	Has difficulty delegating
Motivated, goal oriented	Unable to relax/let go of thinking about work
Has high standards	Self-critical, unable to accept external criticism
Detail oriented	Perfectionistic
Confronts challenges, persists	Ignores emotions of self and others
Accomplishes, gets the job done	Alienates others in the process

CONNECTORS

Connectors, by contrast, find meaning in their relationships with others. They experience joy through emotionally intimate relationships—specifically, deep and personal ties with family and friends.

Being connected to people in this deep and meaningful way is a good thing. Individuals in healthy relationships with others tend to have higher levels of happiness, manage stress better, and live longer.[1] They also tend to have better physical health and experience less loneliness and other negative emotions.[2]

Creating deep relationships requires time, energy, and attention to others' emotions and needs, and Connectors are willing to make the investment. Practically all of us feel some need to belong, but Connectors are better than average at relating to others, and they expend more effort in the process. Connectors share their feelings more openly than most people. Often social, outgoing, and extroverted, Connectors gain energy from being with others and experience warm feelings from togetherness. They seek to be of service to others and to make good friends, the kind of friends that stick with you in the bad times as well as the good.

However, sometimes the need for connection can be taken too far. Some Connectors may be overly dependent on relationships in order to feel fulfilled. Building their identity on their relationships, they can become people pleasers and approval seekers, placing themselves last in an effort to connect with others. Their self-worth comes to depend on the judgment of others. Praise and recognition keeps them feeling well, but perceived or anticipated rejection can overwhelm them with negative feelings.

Jessica, as a Connector, considers her family and friends extremely important. Her friends would say she is approachable, patient, supportive, and thoughtful with them. Jessica has empathy, and she can understand her friends' feelings and respond to their emotional needs. Her good sense of humor and fun-loving nature make it easy to be drawn to her and value her friendship. These are the very traits that originally attracted Michael. Her connectability brought them together despite his lack of ability in this area.

Here are some of the potentially helpful and unhelpful traits of Connectors:

CHARACTERISTICS OF CONNECTORS	
HELPFUL	**UNHELPFUL**
Desires to belong	May become people pleaser
Encouraging, supportive	Tries too hard, overextends self
Builds relationships	Has difficulty saying no
Assists others	Can put others first, neglecting self
Receives help and support from others	Overly concerned with what others think
Has sense of belonging, security, safety	Loses identity in group, poor boundaries
Happier, healthier, less stressed	May have unrealistic expectations for relationships

ACHIEVERS AND CONNECTORS IN RELATIONSHIPS

Like almost everyone, both Achievers and Connectors may have difficulty understanding those who are different from themselves. Similarly, most people, but especially Achievers, don't realize how much effort should be invested in their marriage, which should be their most valuable relationship. Achievers and Connectors both typically have good intentions for their relationship but are unaware of how to achieve them together.

Frankly, Achievers start at a disadvantage when it comes to all relationships. They're simply not that interested in connecting with others to begin with. Often in an A/C marriage, we see the Connecter picking up the slack to maintain relationships with family and friends. The Connector is the one who remembers birthdays and anniversaries, sending cards and gifts and touching base by phone on behalf of both of them. It's not unusual in an A/C marriage for a Connector to have a closer relationship with the Achiever's family than does the Achiever himself or herself.

The Connector may become frustrated by his or her inability to connect as desired with his or her Achiever spouse. The Achiever typically doesn't see the problem and may be threatened by any suggestion from their well-meaning spouse that something's wrong. Most Achievers aren't willing to seriously listen to, understand, and address their Connector partner's concerns early in the process of counseling. The Connector then begins to compensate by seeking additional connection outside of the marriage relationship, and the spouses grow further apart.

This is essentially what happened to Michael and Jessica. As an Achiever, Michael invested nearly all of his time and energy into work and productivity. He worked long hours in his surgical practice and frequently brought practice-related tasks home. Michael didn't see the need to spend much time with Jessica and didn't appreciate it when she suggested his working so much was a problem. In fact, Michael used work and sheer busyness as a method of coping and avoiding arguments with Jessica about his working too much. His response to her complaints that he worked too much was to work more in order to see her less! It was very easy for Michael to justify this because being a surgeon was so much of his identity.

Jessica didn't know exactly how to handle this situation and began to meet her desire for connection by investing in other relationships. She became deeply involved with the children's activities, her small business, the fitness community, friends, and family. You know the rest of the story.

The story of Michael and Jessica illustrates these issues, which are common to the Power Failure Syndrome in A/C marriages. At some point in their marriage, both Michael and Jessica knew things weren't working out like they had expected and wanted. But they couldn't talk about it, work through the issues, and solve the problem. Many A/C couples find themselves in this situation at some time in their relationship. Perhaps you are in this situation yourself.

So how do A/C couples repair rifts and create a fulfilling relationship? The first step is awareness, recognition by both partners that a problem exists. Next comes an understanding of the differences between Achievers and Connectors and a willingness to address the issues. Finally, through individual and mutual work on themselves and their relationship, respectively, perhaps in therapy, couples do develop the marriage they both want.

> Your spouse is different from you and likely has expectations of your relationship that differ from yours.

Unfortunately, many A/C couples never resolve the issues that drive them apart, preferring to simply separate. Achievers have a special difficulty admitting problems or seeking help in their lives. The Connector spouse is much more able to acknowledge the relationship issues and seek help than is the Achiever spouse. But these barriers can be overcome. Read on.

ACHIEVER/ACHIEVER AND CONNECTOR/ CONNECTOR RELATIONSHIPS

An Achiever/Achiever marriage can be a high-stress relationship. Achievers are leaders operating from a "never quit" mindset and are focused on accomplishment, achieving goals, problem solving, and competition. They can be impatient, critical, perfectionistic, and typically have limited awareness of their emotions and effect of their behaviors on others. Since both partners are Achievers, it's unlikely that either will seek help for their relationship issues.

When both spouses are Achievers, the marriage can morph into a competition rather than a cooperative effort. Spouses may keep score in the relationship on who's right or wrong, or each may seek to solve problems by imposing his or her solution on the other. They may have conflict over who's in charge and often choose to operate independently of each other instead of cooperatively. If divorce comes, it can be a messy and acrimonious competition where each seeks to win, either financially or in the eyes of society.

Even if they avoid outright competition, the lack of emotional intimacy in an Achiever/Achiever marriage can still create problems. In this case the relationship may be operated as more of a business partnership than a marriage. Feelings are minimized and the couple just sticks to the facts. Dinner conversation is about the big business deal rather than family dynamics. The dual Achiever couple may outsource childrearing to nannies and boarding schools, and the children may feel closer to the nanny than their own mother and father. If divorce comes, it's a simple and low-key business deal to split the marital assets and move on.

Connectors, on the other hand, are more ready for intimate relationships. We feel that the Connector/Connector couple has the best chance, from the beginning, to establish a mutually satisfying relationship. Connectors value conversation, interaction, and intimacy, which are vital to a fulfilling relationship, though in any marriage conflicts will occur. Resolving conflicts positively is essential, and simply being a Connector does not guarantee possessing good conflict resolution skills. They may be too anxious or fearful of the effect on the relationship to effectively deal with marital issues. However, in general, Connectors are much more willing to acknowledge difficulties and seek help when necessary, which is a very good thing.

This overview of the typical dynamics of the A/A couple and the C/C couple is brief because the Achiever/Achiever couple is not very likely to be interested in relationship advice, and the Connector/Connector couple is not likely to need it.

THE BOTTOM LINE:

- People are different. Your spouse is different from you and likely has expectations of your relationship that differ from yours.
- If you are an Achiever, or are married to one, building a strong marriage may be difficult, but it is possible if you can exchange some traits that are keys to your success in business for those that more useful at home.
- Either way, you can have the relationship you want if both parties are willing to work for it.

Recognize your differences *and work to connect* with your spouse.

Better Together

Discover the Essentials of a Strong Marriage

THE ESSENTIALS FOR A STRONG MARRIAGE

How hard is it to get married? It's not too hard from a procedural standpoint. Register with the county, pay a fee, and find an official to tie the knot. Just about any couple can make it happen. Unfortunately, not everyone is ready to do it well. We know that we weren't.

Marriage isn't rocket science, but it does take work to create a lasting and vibrant relationship, and there are some important things that you may not know, even after many years together. The factors necessary to creating a strong bond with your spouse can be distilled down to five key principles:

1. **Partnership of Equals:** You participate as an equal partner in your marriage and take responsibility for (and only for) your own feelings, thoughts, and actions.
2. **Marriage Is a Priority:** You are fully engaged, committed, and make the relationship with your spouse a high priority.
3. **Effective Communication and Conflict Resolution:** You strive to communicate effectively and to constructively manage and resolve conflicts.
4. **Forgiveness:** You are willing to forgive and work to rebuild and maintain trust.

5. **Intimacy:** You strive for physical and emotional intimacy with your spouse.

PARTNERSHIP OF EQUALS

All these critical principles begin with you. Not your spouse or both of you together; just you. This is often the hardest lesson to learn. You should be an equal partner with your spouse, neither seeking control over his or her behavior nor giving up control over your own actions. At this point, it's

> The best way to bring about a change in your spouse's behavior is to change your own.

important to clarify that we are not talking about an equal delegation or distribution of work duties, for example parenting, in the marriage. Rather, we mean an equal personal responsibility as adult partners in the marriage relationship.

Any attempts to control or change your spouse will not help your marriage. On the contrary, doing so almost guarantees the marriage will go wrong. A relationship, by definition, consists of the interaction between people and depends on the behavior of each party. If you want a strong marriage, you must be prepared to change yourself. Thinking that your spouse is the problem and trying to fix him or her won't help your relationship. Sure, your spouse may have issues, but you probably do too. Change has to start in you.

Michael and Jessica are a good example of a couple trying to change each other and not themselves. Michael could justify and rationalize his excessive work focus by blaming Jessica for spending too much money. Jessica justified her time at the fitness center and spending by noting Michael's limited involvement and presence with the family. Michael was never compelled to increase his social or emotional awareness to become a more well-rounded person, because Jessica assumed this responsibility.

It seems paradoxical, but the best way to bring about a change in your spouse's behavior is to change your own. Trying to force others to change only creates resistance on their part and drains precious time and energy that could be channeled into changing yourself. Focus only on controlling your own thoughts and actions. When one partner is truly focused on becoming the best person that he or she can be, quite often the spouse decides to change too.

Not only should you not try to control your spouse, you also must not relinquish control of yourself. This is part of being an equal partner. If you are passive and avoid responsibility by allowing your spouse to inappropriately control aspects of your life, you are participating in the same dysfunctional unequal controlling relationship from the other side. Achievers tend to seek control over situations and/or people, while Connectors may too readily relinquish control to maintain peace in the relationship. Neither approach works.

Dysfunctional people tend to attract dysfunctional partners, which can produce a problematic relationship. Eventually these individuals are faced with either allowing their relationship to remain dysfunctional or changing to resolve their own issues. The good news is that the reverse is also true—emotionally healthy people attract emotionally healthy partners. By avoiding blame, maintaining responsibility for yourself, and growing emotionally, you prepare a solid foundation for a lasting marriage.

MARRIAGE IS A PRIORITY

Principle number two states that you are engaged and fully committed to the relationship and that it's a priority. But how high of a priority should it be? That's up to you, but if you want a strong marriage, then it's going to have to be more important than your job, the kids, the in-laws, hobbies, and just about everything else in your life.

Michael and Jessica didn't hold their marriage as the highest priority. In fact, their relationship often just got the scraps—whatever energy they had left over at the end of the day. Typically, that wasn't too much. Most of the time they were physically and emotionally exhausted from the day; nothing was left to give to the other and to the relationship. This is pretty common in A/C relationships in today's hectic society. While Achievers single-mindedly drive toward "success," Connectors may try to make everyone happy and overextend themselves outside of their spousal relationship.

> Forgiveness is a choice of the forgiver. It's not about the other person's response; it's about letting go.

Although infidelity is a common, serious cause of divorce, more than 50 percent of divorces are caused by issues seemingly of lesser severity, such as growing apart, incompatibility, personality clashes, or poor communication.[1] Ideally, your marriage should be more important than your work, extended family, and even your children. However, it should *not* be more important than *everything* else. Your own spiritual and emotional wellness is vital to creating and maintaining a fulfilling relationship with your spouse.

Let us explain. At first, this may sound selfish or like we have it backward, but marriage works best when the participants are spiritually and emotionally well people. As flight attendants teach in the case of an in-flight airplane decompression, you must take your own oxygen first before trying to assist others. We are not talking about putting your superficial wants ahead of your marriage, rather asserting that your own nurturing and growth as an individual person must come first. Marriage is not meant to stifle or suppress you as an individual.

As an example of what we mean, it's common for recovering drug addicts or alcoholics to put their sobriety as a higher priority than their marriage. Their reasoning is that if they aren't committed to sobriety and fall back into active substance abuse again, the marriage is at risk. We agree. In general, we can say that your own personal physical, spiritual, and emotional health should be your first priority and that your marriage should be next in line.

EFFECTIVE COMMUNICATION AND CONFLICT RESOLUTION

Effective communication and conflict resolution are critical. You're living with this other person 24/7 and, hopefully, happily ever after. How's that going to work if you can't talk through disagreements and settle them without enmity? In every marriage there will be hundreds or even thousands of disagreements during the years you are together. Conflicts in marriage, like death and taxes, are a given. But a difference in opinion doesn't always have to be a negative. Resolving difficult issues in healthy and productive ways often brings partners closer.

> By forgiving, you release yourself from the misery that you have allowed past events to create in your life now.

Both Achievers and Connectors may have difficulties in this area. Achievers, competitive by nature, simply want to win the argument. While Connectors, valuing the relationship more than winning, may give in too quickly, only to walk away with lingering resentment.

Some couples, perhaps most, even create their own conflict. Many individuals keep score in their marriage, constantly measuring their partner's performance against their own perceived contributions. And, of course, the scorekeeper usually counts him or herself ahead. Naturally, it's easier to find fault in others than to accept fault in yourself. This kind of scorekeeping creates constant tension and conflict in the relationship. The key is to avoid *creating* conflict when possible and to try to resolve conflict when it arises.

Michael and Jessica had real problems here, either shutting down to avoid arguing or lashing out and exploding in anger. Neither of these is helpful. Ideally, partners can talk about the issue or behavior creating the tension and express their feelings to each other without shutting down or blowing up. "I" statements, such as, "I get frustrated when you interrupt me," are most helpful in this context. Being able to constructively express your thoughts and feelings, without blame, is one of the most important abilities in avoiding problems from unresolved conflict. Solving marital conflict is similar to tackling other life challenges. Research supports that strengthening problem-solving skills is critical to successful management of life's stressors and increasing marital stability.[2, 3] Like exercising a muscle in the gym, facing conflict squarely and working through the pain helps you grow emotionally and makes the relationship stronger. And just like avoiding exercise causes muscles to atrophy, avoiding conflict because it's painful at the time of disagreement (which it is) causes your relational problem-solving skills to atrophy. If you fail here, you will begin to develop the frustration that can lead to anger and resentment.

FORGIVENESS

Even with the best communication and conflict resolution, feelings are going to get hurt. Minor slights will be common and major transgressions may happen, too. That's where forgiveness and building trust come in. Forgiving your spouse is not just for his or her benefit! It's for *your* benefit and for the benefit of the relationship.[4] Forgiving allows you to let go of anger and bypass the resentment that will surely build if you bottle up your anger inside.

This is not to say that all of your spouse's actions are tolerable or acceptable. Michael's affairs are not something that Jessica should tolerate. However, if she hopes to have a happy future with Michael, she will need to be able to forgive (not forget) his past transgressions, just as Michael will need to forgive her emotional separation from him to focus on her work and the children. At this point in their story, we're not sure if that's going to happen.

Forgiveness is the ability to release the emotional pain that was caused by another's actions, without necessarily condoning the behavior. It enables the person who has been hurt to achieve personal healing, even if they choose not to maintain the relationship. This does not require an apology or repentance from the wrongdoer, although it may be easier if that occurs. Forgiveness is a choice of the forgiver. It's not about the other person's response; it's about letting go of the internal pain.

Some people have an easier time forgiving than others. Achiever or Connector, your ability to forgive may be based more on your experiences growing up and in prior relationships than your personality. However Achievers, because of their high personal standards, may find it more difficult to forgive themselves than others. Connectors may struggle with forgiving others because they feel they have invested so much in the relationship. Everyone can learn to forgive.

Of course, most people can't forgive others instantly, especially for major hurts. On the other hand, time alone does not result in forgiveness. Forgiving is an active process, and it takes effort. But it's worth the work. There is tremendous power and healing in forgiveness. By forgiving, you release yourself from the misery that you have allowed past events to create in your life now.

The decision to forgive also resets a person's ability to trust, to be vulnerable with others, and to pursue relationship-constructive rather than relationship-destructive actions.[5] Even if Michael and Jessica end up divorcing, it will still be important for them to forgive each other, so that they don't take their unresolved anger, hurt, and sadness into any future relationships.

INTIMACY

Achieving close physical and emotional intimacy with your spouse is harder than it seems. Achievers and Connectors have different behavioral styles. Much has been written about different personality styles in relationships, and you may be familiar with this general topic. For example, in *Men Are from Mars, Women Are from Venus*,[6] Dr. John

Gray describes the uniqueness of men and women as they relate to each other verbally and emotionally. He emphasizes that in essence we speak different languages and need to understand these differences in order to get along better. Although his ideas are controversial, we believe Dr. Gray's book became a bestseller because readers recognize an essential truth in his message.

Another book emphasizing our differences is *The Five Love Languages*[7] by Dr. Gary Chapman. In it, he shares five different ways in which individuals experience, express, and receive love. Some prefer a fantastic meal or completed project, others prefer positive affirmations or gifts, and still others prefer physical affection. The point is—we're not all the same. What your partner needs and wants is not the same as what you desire. So we need to speak in the other's language in order to get our message across. Partners might be doing wonderful things for each other, but if it's not what gives the other a sense of being loved, not much is gained. When you understand your mate, you'll be able to connect better and energize your marriage.

Making allowances for the differences between you and your spouse—Achiever or Connector—is critical, because in our view, physical intimacy (including sex) is necessary for emotional intimacy. The sexless marriage does not have a good prognosis.[8] On the other hand, emotional intimacy is also an important precursor to physical intimacy.[9] This can lead to a common A/C marriage chicken-and-egg problem. The Connector desires emotional intimacy before sexual intimacy, while the more emotionally disconnected Achiever can be helped to open up emotionally following a sexual interaction. This is a more significant problem for couples when the Achiever is a man and the Connecter a woman.

This common marital issue is best treated with flexibility. Understand that your spouse is different from you, and be prepared to move a little in his or her direction.

How are you doing with the five essentials of a healthy marriage? Please take the following self-assessment to help you understand yourself in the context of your relationship.

SELF-ASSESSMENT—MARRIAGE ESSENTIALS

Answer these questions for yourself. You may wish to write down the answers.

1. I participate as an equal partner in our marriage and take responsibility for (and only for) my own thoughts and actions.

   - Do I try to change my partner?

   - Am I open to hearing my spouse's views and not just my own?

   - Do I find myself justifying my actions or blaming others?

2. I am fully engaged, committed, and make the relationship with my spouse a priority.

   - What are the top priorities in my life?

   - What things take away from time with my spouse?

   - Do I ever feel guilty about not spending more time with my mate?

   - Does my spouse want more of my time than I am willing to give? Why?

3. I strive to communicate effectively and to constructively resolve conflict.

   - How well do I communicate with my spouse?

- Do I find myself finishing my partner's sentences and constantly interrupting?
- Are there issues that are hard to talk about . . . things that I am reluctant to bring up, or don't want to discuss when he or she brings them up for discussion?
- How often do we actually achieve lasting, satisfactory conflict resolution?
- Do I ever refuse to talk about a subject?

4. I am willing to forgive and work to build trust.

- Am I nursing a grudge? Holding on to resentment?
- Have I worked at forgiveness? Do I know how?
- How often do I or my partner use the silent treatment with each other?
- What prevents me from forgiving?

5. I aim for physical and emotional intimacy.

- Have I found that physical intimacy is more satisfying when I'm emotionally connected?
- How do I initiate and experience emotional intimacy?
- How are emotional and physical intimacy connected for me?
- What did emotional intimacy look like for me as I was growing up?

Did this exercise help you see where you stand? Sometimes it's not obvious, particularly if you are minimizing or exaggerating issues. It can be hard to be completely honest with yourself. We recommend asking your spouse to answer the questions too, and then suggest you get together and talk through your answers.

Maybe you're not doing so well on some of these marriage essentials. That's normal, especially in today's society where so many destructive forces can make it tough to form and maintain strong relationships.

THE BOTTOM LINE:

- Marriage doesn't come naturally for most people, especially Achievers. Achiever or Connector, you will need to make an effort to have a lasting and loving marriage.
- Your marriage must be a higher priority than your work, children, and friends.
- Relationships, by definition, are not all about you. Your spouse is a separate person with separate needs, wants, and feelings. Learn what makes your spouse feel loved.
- You will need to change yourself for the better to have better relationships.

Personal responsibility powers *healthy relationships.*

Life Can Be a Battlefield

Keep Love Alive

The environment in which you live can shape your thinking and behavior in ways that can be hard to recognize. Our current culture is hostile to intimate relationships. Yes, people have always struggled in relationships, but life seems different in the information age. Now more than ever, the prevailing culture is unfriendly to marriages and long-term relationships in two main ways. One is the implicit message that material success is more important than success in relationships. The second is the sheer busyness and fragmentation of contemporary life.

Relationships: Undervalued, but Key to Happiness

Our society overvalues success in business, politics, athletics, fame, and fortune while undervaluing success in relationships.[1] This is a prioritization problem. Unfortunately, marriage is not a top priority for many couples. The world's definition of success comes first.

In the quest for the good life, many people pursue power and control to achieve material success. In the process, they can develop an obsession with work and productivity. Their mantra seems to be, "If you work hard, you can achieve anything." They seem to assume that gaining status and wealth will result in lifelong happiness and joy. Of course, it doesn't work that way. A person with wealth is not guaranteed joy any more (or less) than a person of different means. As Mother Teresa said, "Even the rich are hungry for love, for being cared for, for being wanted, for having someone to call their own."

If this is you, recognize it for what it is, but don't place all the blame on yourself. Analyze the messages sent through advertising and other media. Advertising's goal is to get you to do one thing—buy the product. How many products are associated with success in your mind? Where did that association come from? Were you born knowing that a certain kind of house, brand of car, style of wristwatch, or ink pen meant success? If not, where did you learn that?

Who are heroes in our society? Typically, they're high-profile, high-income, hard-driving, and high-achievement people—business or political leaders, famous and wealthy athletes, or Hollywood stars.

Business books are written by and about great leaders (often men) who have created enormous wealth for themselves and their shareholders. Nobody asks each man's wife if he was a great husband, nor do they ask the children if he was a great dad. It's the same story with Hollywood actresses and actors. Many celebrities continue to be lionized despite a trail of broken relationships with spouses and children. When did you last read a book or newspaper headline about a person whose most outstanding achievement was their solid relationship with their spouse and children? It doesn't happen often, except perhaps in the obituary section.

> Happiness and success in life really come from meaningful work in the service of others.

Now think about your hometown heroes. Who are the unsung people making a difference in the lives of others every day? Teachers, nurses, military personnel, firefighters, police officers, clergy, and social workers, to name a few. Good fathers and mothers and caring wives and husbands are on that list, too. All these individuals take their roles and relationships with others seriously. They don't do it for money or fame, but most love their work because it's fulfilling. The truth is that happiness and success in life really come from meaningful work in the service of others.

Research backs this up. In her book *The How of Happiness*, Dr. Sonja Lyubomirsky concludes that very wealthy people are not much happier than average folks. In fact, she found that not only does materialism *not* produce happiness, but rather it's a strong predictor of *unhappiness*.[2] Psychologist David Myers says that money doesn't make people happy, noting ". . . our becoming much better off over the last four decades has not been accompanied by one iota of increased subjective well-being."[3]

Organizing your life around the pursuit of wealth and power can be a prescription for depression. Dr. Tim Kasser, author of *The High Price of Materialism,* finds that individuals choosing money, image, and popularity as their primary goals have less life satisfaction, experience fewer positive emotions, and report more depression and anxiety than those who have very little money, possessions, and status.[4] Collectively, these and other studies, along with the direct experience of many individuals, are fueling a growing movement for simplifying life. Individuals are waking up from the American dream and deciding to focus more on seeking meaning and better relationships, rather than more money and material goods.

Are you able to identify with this from your own experience? Over your lifetime, you probably have experienced varying levels of material comfort and worldly success. Reflect upon this for a minute. Did any of those changes in your material status create any more or less underlying happiness in you as a person? In our cases, the answer is no. Dr. Weiss was just as happy as a medical student in a one-bedroom apartment as he is now living in a two-story house, and Dr. Ferretti recalls the happy time during his internship when all of his worldly possessions could fit in his beat-up Ford Escort.

Many of us are lured into thinking that the more we have or accomplish, the happier we will be. We can wind up chasing money, possessions, or experiences in an attempt to be fulfilled. Maybe you've seen the bumper sticker, "Whoever dies with the most toys wins." Of course, the bumper sticker is a joke, but it expresses a fundamental truth about how many behave in our materialistic culture. It is easy to believe that more stuff will make you happy, but think it over. The more you have, the more you want, and the more stress you experience trying to protect your stuff. Give some thought to your personal history and perhaps you will get a sense of the degree to which this applies to you.

In our culture, it is all too easy to be captivated by the American Dream and its toxic focus on more stuff, while losing sight of the value of your relationships. Achievers buy big-ticket items without flinching—boats, cars, the latest consumer electronics—because they believe they're worth it and they want others to believe this, too. Connectors may overspend, not so much to reward themselves but rather to strengthen connections with family and friends. Since each is pursuing a different dream of success, neither completely understands their motivation or the basic drives of their spouse. And neither has identified the true value in their marriage or how to cultivate it.

Use the following self-assessment to help you better understand your orientation around people and possessions.

SELF-ASSESSMENT—PEOPLE VS. POSSESSIONS

Which would I value more:

- Enjoying a "power lunch" with business acquaintances in an expensive restaurant, or a casual lunch with a close friend in a neighborhood diner?
- Shopping by myself in an upscale department store, or hanging out with friends at the local mall?

- Retiring at age sixty without a family while cashing out millions in stock options, or having a modest retirement income while enjoying a close relationship with my children and grandchildren who live nearby?
- Spending the day fishing alone in an expensive boat, or fishing from a seawall with a couple of buddies?
- Living with my spouse in a penthouse condo with no friends in the building, or in a modest house in a neighborhood full of friends and relatives?

The truth is that having close relationships with others is one of the keys to happiness and fulfillment. Most people learn this eventually, but some never do. Learning it earlier in life helps a lot, but changing course at any age makes a big difference.

CONTEMPORARY LIFE: ULTRA-BUSY AND FRAGMENTED

Life used to be different, not necessarily better, but definitely different—slower, simpler, and more restrained. Relationships were often forced on people by their circumstances. They lived in the same town they grew up in. They worked for the same company as their neighbors, attended the same house of worship, and ate at the same local restaurants. That's just the way it was.

Things have changed. Society has evolved dramatically over the past few decades, both technologically and interpersonally. The Internet, mobile phones, and other advances in communications have changed our culture, including the way we relate to each other. We can work and live in cities a hundred miles or more apart. Where we grew up no longer determines our destiny. We have the ability to access information and people in an instant. Likewise, people and information attempt to reach us in an instant.

E-mail, social networking, instant messages, and phone calls can create a constant stimulus-and-response lifestyle. At one point, the promise of advanced technology was to free up time and create more opportunity for leisure. Instead, it seems like just the opposite has happened. Many people seem to have almost no down time, and the constant connection causes disconnection from the people closest to them. This can feed into the Achiever's drive for productivity, and Connectors may spend too much time connecting on social media while connecting too little at home. Regardless of personality, these new technologies can be addicting.

Consider the case of Kyle and his wife, Sandy.

> Kyle had always been an early adopter of new technology and the latest personal communication devices, and working in the IT field reinforced that habit. At first, Sandy appreciated Kyle's dedication to keeping up with the fast-paced tech world, but gradually the devices seemed to take over. It got to the point that Kyle seemed to spend most of his waking hours online via computer, smartphone, or other high-tech gadget.
>
> Then he entered the world of multiplayer online gaming, which quickly became all consuming. Essentially, Kyle's avatar became more important than Kyle's life. With no time for connection and conversation, his relationship with Sandy steadily deteriorated. When her attempts to address the situation were rebuffed, Sandy wondered if Kyle had met someone else online.
>
> Eventually Kyle agreed to counseling after Sandy refused to discuss having children without a change in the relationship.

This example is not unusual. Many couples are becoming more disconnected as one or both turn to an online world and escape from the real world. But the real world is still there, and your real relationships pay the price for your many online relationships. The unusual part of Kyle and Sandy's story is that they were willing to seek counseling before divorce or other crisis. Many couples aren't.

As far as work is concerned, while technology has freed us from our desks, it has chained us to our jobs. We are always at work now, anytime and anywhere. We have higher expectations of technology and each other, and have become intolerant of glitches in the system. With these changes come increased impatience and frustration with even minor delays and mishaps. What do you think when you send an e-mail and don't get a response within a day? Or maybe within the hour?

> Good relationships require presence and focused attention to the other person.

These advances in electronic communications only feed our culture of overachievement. Many of us are trying to juggle work, maintain the home, shop, raise children, plus manage hobbies, movies, sports, school, vacations, and the children's activities. And how are we doing? Not well, and we know it. A majority of Americans would be willing to take a proportional pay cut for one day a week off from work.[5]

Perhaps they want that extra day to sleep. More than 60 percent of Americans sleep less than seven hours per night on average in spite of the fact that almost all adults need seven or more hours for optimal health. Sleep deprivation impairs memory, increases levels of stress hormones, disrupts the body's normal metabolism, increases the risk of motor vehicle accidents, and may even lead to premature aging. How do you and your spouse get along when you're both overtired?

All of these changes inhibit the development of meaningful relationships. Good relationships require presence and focused attention to the other person. By this, we mean a deep connectedness and understanding of the other person, including an emotional connection. Understand and appreciate their feelings, and let them connect with the real you. This takes time, and who has it? How could we have the time with the busyness and fragmentation of our lives?

The following self-assessment can help you gauge your attention to relationships.

SELF-ASSESSMENT—ATTENDING TO RELATIONSHIPS

These questions are designed to help you gain a better understanding of how contemporary life may be affecting your ability to maintain close relationships.

- Have you ever been with someone who is text messaging during your meeting? How did that feel?
- Can you tell during a telephone conversation if the other party is answering their e-mail or watching TV while talking with you? How do you sense that?
- Have you ever tried to talk with your spouse when he or she is stressed out and in a hurry? How did that go?
- Have you ever been the one to do any of the things just mentioned? How do you think the other person felt?

Reflect on your answers. Perhaps you might discuss them with a friend or your spouse. Do you see how distractions can harm connection? And it's almost impossible not to be constantly distracted in contemporary life.

Some will argue that we are more connected through technology—that social networking has been good for relationships. This is not true, at least not in terms of intimate *personal* relationships that build marriages. The technologies themselves are not the issue; it's how they are used. Although hundreds of millions of people are connected on the Internet, how deep are those connections?

Facebook and similar sites can be wonderful ways for close family and friends to stay connected. No more snail mailing pictures of the grandchildren. Grandma and grandpa get to see the latest photos and perhaps even a video online. Then perhaps they pick up the phone to chat about it. Skype video conferencing is an excellent way for distant relatives to stay connected. An army officer, on deployment in a war zone, can still read a bedtime story to her kids! Clearly, technology can be used to help relationships.

But this is not how most people use most technology. For example, how many people's Facebook friends are mere acquaintances, or less than acquaintances? How many Facebook posts represent heartfelt communication? Shorter posts can be very superficial. Sharing small snippets of our lives with many is no substitute for deep, intimate, or meaningful connections. When was the last time you sat down with a friend for an intimate conversation over a cup of coffee? When did you last pour your heart out to another about something troubling you (in person, by phone, or by Skype)? And when did you last spend an uninterrupted day or weekend with family and friends?

Electronic messaging (EM) isn't the same as a face-to-face meeting or even a telephone conversation. This is because approximately 90 percent of communication is not linked to the actual words used.

> **Time Is Your Most Valuable Gift**
> You can earn more money or you can live on less, but you can't create time. You can't slow it down. When a day is gone, it's gone. And time, not money, is what your family and friends need from you. Relationships require spending time together. Spend time with the people you love. Think presence, not presents.

More than half comes from body language, and most of the remainder can be linked to volume, pitch, and rhythm. Only 10 percent or so of the total message is derived from the words themselves.[6] We read others' intentions and make a connection not only by what they say, but more importantly, by their body language, facial expression, and tone of voice. With electronic conversations, we aren't able to communicate and bond with others nearly as effectively. Were you ever offended by an e-mail that someone else intended as a joke?

Most people don't need *more* social network connections or Facebook friends. They would be better off with *deeper* connections with those they should be closest with—their spouse, their children, and their real friends. It's the depth and meaning found in relationships that brings joy to life. So how do you do that?

First, recognize the issue, and be intentional in scheduling time for face-to-face interactions. If you don't make the time, it won't happen. You needn't get together just for conversation if that's not comfortable for you.

Try an activity—fishing, golf, a shared meal, or a joint project— anything to bring you together with the others you care about.

Be kind to yourself, and set better boundaries to intrusions. Don't let the world control your most valuable resource—your time. Leave work at work and set a limited block of time for chores over the weekend. Focus on having fun with and connecting to people. Try setting aside six hours each weekend to disconnect and spend time playing, talking, and sharing other activities with your family and friends. During this disconnect time, all electronics get turned off, and people get tuned in.

CONTEMPORARY LIFE: COMPLEX, CONFUSING, AND SCARY

Contemporary life is not just busy, it's also complicated. And dealing with this complexity reduces time for important relationships. As the amount of information available goes up, the amount you need or seem to need does too.

Think about managing electronic business accounts. How many user IDs and passwords do you have? Twenty? Fifty? How many did your parents have when they were your age? And how are you at troubleshooting computer performance problems? Many people cannot do this, and trying often makes them feel completely inadequate.

Or what about raising children—parenting, discipline, homework, childcare options, college choices? There's a lot to master, and much of the learning is experiential in nature. The best way to be good at parenting is to have done it once already! Many of us muddle through but look back with regret about parenting lessons learned only after the kids are grown.

Life can also be confusing. Within the contemporary era, family roles are often uncertain and every couple must determine their own job and family expectations and arrangements. It used to be that the man went to work as the breadwinner and the woman managed the home and family as the housewife. We're not defending it, but it was predictable and everyone knew what was expected, like it or not.

In today's world we are no longer constrained by old society-defined roles, so many couples struggle to adapt to new roles and identities. Dual-income households or working moms partnered with stay-at-home dads are part of this shift. Benefits include financial gain for families and opportunities for personal growth outside the home. Unfortunately, many spouses don't come to an agreement on their respective roles and how to cooperate within the family.

> Expectations do not always translate into behavior.

When both partners work, often the wife expects her husband will help more with the housework and childcare. She expects to share responsibility and authority in the household on all matters, including finances, parenting, and household management. In reality, this rarely happens. Studies consistently show that when both spouses work full time, the wife still shoulders the majority of the housework and child caretaking chores.[7,8] Significant conflict can occur when the wife expects an equal workload while the husband expects traditional household roles to continue. *Expectations do not always translate into behavior.*

Role confusion can also happen in the transition from work to home. Perhaps, as an Achiever at the office, you are in charge, making decisions, delegating, and generally commanding others. Arriving home in the evening, you may have trouble recognizing you're now half of a two-person partnership. Or you bring home that competitive business attitude, which helped you rise through the ranks at work, and use it when you deal with family issues. But you're not in competition with your spouse. Your title at home should be partner, not boss.

Michael had real problems here. Like many Achievers, he frequently brought the office home with him, either in his briefcase or his head. His hospital persona and behavior—highly skilled surgeon, lifesaver, and taskmaster—came along too. Some days Jessica wondered how his head could fit through the door, his ego was so inflated. He expected Jessica and the boys to praise, serve, and admire him the way his staff did. And of course that didn't happen.

It is common for spouses never to identify and talk through their expectations or to agree upon their respective responsibilities in the family. Most do not address these issues prior to marriage, but some learn to do so over time. Indeed, the ability to proactively discuss expectations and desires and to negotiate roles is important throughout marriage, since they are continually in flux.

In addition to facing complexity and confusion, many people live in a perpetual state of mild to moderate anxiety or fear. The contemporary world may really be a more dangerous world in some ways, but the 24/7 news cycle fosters fear through sensational news coverage.[9] A memorable snapshot feature in *USA Today*[10] listed the five greatest concerns parents and teachers had about children in the 1950s: talking out of turn, chewing gum in class, doing homework, stepping out of line, and cleaning their rooms. Then the newspaper article listed the five top concerns of parents today: drug addiction, teenage pregnancy, suicide and homicide, gang violence, and anorexia and bulimia. Without doubt, fundamental issues of parenting and family life have changed radically. Sharing fears can be hard for anyone, but Achievers may be especially reluctant to share their fears, perceiving a potential for loss of status or reputation, or an unwillingness to seem weak. Connectors might be more open to sharing but find that their Achiever spouses don't respond in a supportive manner, instead dismissing or minimizing the issues. But when partners can't be open with each other, the buried emotions add to the stress of the marriage. Without a constructive way to release the fear, some individuals may even turn to destructive stress reducers such as alcohol/drugs, sex, food, or other addictions.

The following self-assessment can help you see how the complexity, confusion, and fears that can come with modern life are affecting your relationships.

SELF-ASSESSMENT—CONNECTING OR DISCONNECTING

- Have you had a meaningful conversation with your partner about roles and responsibilities?
- How often do you work on tasks jointly and discuss expectations?
- Have you shared your feelings openly about your own role in the family?
- Have you discussed how best to raise your children? Do you agree with each other on this?
- Are you working as a team in raising your children and running the household?
- Do you ever feel like there are two separate entities in your marriage, each striving for different goals?

Reflect on your answers.

CONTEMPORARY LIFE: USE ONCE AND DISCARD

When the pressure builds and relationships suffer, another tenet of contemporary life surfaces: disposability. Single-use products have become the norm; we are accustomed to discarding many common items after just one use. We now routinely use disposable dinnerware, cameras, razors, and contact lenses. With technology advancing so quickly, many of our products become outdated almost overnight. When electronic products need repair, it is often less expensive to purchase a new one and discard the broken item. We trade in used cars with plenty of good years left when newer, more exciting models are released. It's easy to slip into a mindset that all products have a limited life expectancy regardless of their functionality.

Could it be that this disposability mindset has slipped into our contemporary view of relationships? Perhaps it's one reason that divorce just seems so ordinary now. People get new spouses all the time. People we read about and people we know. Could an automotive mentality apply here? We might be excited by a "newer model" with more attractive features and decide to trade in our current spouse. Or we might just feel that our current relationship is going to require too much time and trouble to repair. Let's just get a new one, despite our own contribution to the disrepair of our marriage or family relationships. As with cars, relationships require routine maintenance. And when the service schedule is ignored, damage results.

Maybe we get bored, tired of the same old, same old. We might grow weary and restless, seeking more stimulation, arousal, and challenge—especially if that's what we Achievers thrive on at work. For those individuals who operate from a "never good enough" mentality, success may be defined as being with the perfect person and maintaining the perfect image. This can leave their Connector spouses feeling like they're competing against an impossible standard and that nothing they do is good enough. Some will give up trying, only to detach instead.

The reality is that all marriages require regular, consistent attention and preventive maintenance. Many who don't learn this the first time and experience a Power Failure will go on to repeat the pattern more than once. As the same cycle of frustration, anger, resentment, and detachment occurs in their new relationship, they once again blame their partner and look for the exit door.

THE BOTTOM LINE:

- Today's society may be working against you in many ways. By idolizing wealth and power, reinforcing disposable relationships, and creating a warp speed activity level, our culture has undermined the foundations of strong relationships—time, attention, and caring.

- We generate much of our own stress and many of our own problems, but we can live differently. Be willing to make difficult choices to strengthen your relationships.

- Create a strong foundation for your marriage. Work and achievement can take over your life if you let them. Schedule time for rest, relaxation, and relationships.

Different
isn't always better,
but better
is always different.

Five Ways to a Power Failure

Avoiding Relationship Ruiners

Could your behavioral style be getting in the way of your relationships? Very likely.

Achievers often exhibit six main personality issues that can interfere with their ability to develop a strong marriage. Connectors may share some of these but are more likely to struggle understanding and coping with these traits in their Achiever spouse. These are:

- Emotional unawareness
- Overly strong achievement drive
- Perfectionism
- Criticizing
- Attempting to control your partner
- Allowing your partner to control you

Before addressing these characteristics one by one, let's consider personality in general. Three controversial questions in psychological circles are: "What is personality? How is it developed? Can personality be changed?"

We define "personality" as "the overall pattern of thoughts, emotions, and behavior expressed in a particular individual." If you want to look it up in a dictionary yourself, you'll find something pretty close to this. Personality is not found in your material possessions, social status, or your job. Personality is how you think, act, and feel. Here are some terms that might be used to describe different components of personality: analytical, active, rational, intelligent, witty, critical, encouraging, emotional, cold, withdrawn, moody, fast-paced, worrier, upbeat, fidgety, aggressive, intense, explosive, temperamental, insecure, sensitive. Each of us has a unique personality that defines who we are and how we relate to our environment. Most often, when you think about someone else, their personality is what you think of as "them."

An individual's personality develops over many years, from childhood into early adulthood. Despite a century or more of studying this, psychologists are

> Baggage from childhood often contributes to disconnection between spouses, holding their relationship back.

still unable to agree on the crucial factors that contribute to our personality as we develop into adults. However, there is general agreement that both genetics and environment (sometimes termed "nature and nurture") play important roles in defining personalities. Just as trees that grow in a windy area are bent over, our personalities are shaped by our parental upbringing and other important childhood experiences.

Importantly, some personality traits can be helpful adaptations to experiences in childhood but be harmful to development of strong relationships in adulthood. For example, in a household filled with conflict, children may become passive and submissive to avoid the arguments. And, of course, in such an environment children experience stress and unpleasant feelings, which they may carry into their adult relationships.

Basically, children have very limited resources and options for coping and just do the best they can under the circumstances. But some of their most effective methods, such as avoidance, withdrawal, and detachment, are not helpful coping strategies for adults. Aggression, belittling, passive-aggressiveness, and control may be even more harmful.

When one or both parents are emotionally and verbally abusive, a child may learn to keep quiet and suppress thoughts and feelings. Children raised in abusive homes may detach or shut down at times of conflict when it would be more helpful to constructively engage their spouse and resolve the issue. Others raised with abuse may overreact, become belligerent, and lash out when differences arise. They may even become physically abusive themselves. Our point is, baggage from childhood often contributes to disconnection between spouses, holding their relationship back.

> If you can resist narrowly defining yourself, you can be freer to explore different behaviors and to enjoy multiple roles, activities, and behaviors.

But . . . can personality be changed? We believe it can. Those bent-over trees are never going to straighten out, but people are not trees. Some will reply, "No, personality is fixed," but agree that aspects of individual personality can be changed. Well, if personality is the totality of its aspects, or traits, and these aspects are changed—then the entire personality is changed!

Yes, a person can change over time.[1, 2] You may know someone who was intense or angry as a younger person but has mellowed with age. Unfortunately, personality can change for the worse, as when some become more angry, bitter, and withdrawn as they nurse grudges over time. Many forces continue to shape our personalities as we move through life, but the most important force that can shape anyone's personality is their own desire to change.

Both authors are examples of personality change. Dr. Weiss is much less driven, temperamental, impatient, inconsiderate, and selfish, and he is much kinder, gentler, more tolerant, and supportive than he used to be. In fact, people meeting him again after a long absence say things like, "You sure have changed" or "You're like a different person."

Dr. Ferretti was shy, timid, and insecure as a child. After the death of his mother when he was thirteen, he made a conscious decision to be different and take action to overcome his shyness. He decided to join the track team in high school to push himself to grow physically and emotionally. Through his high school and college years, he developed more confidence and became more outgoing and assertive with others. Today it's hard to believe that he was once a shy and quiet boy.

In addition, Dr. Ferretti witnesses change every day in his practice. Some clients change a little and some change a lot. Of course, change takes hard work, and very few revamp their entire personality. But, make no mistake; change is possible when the desire and motivation are strong.

Typically, the goal in counseling is to help individuals change just a little bit at first. With time, more significant improvement may be possible. A typical counseling approach would be to tone down or take the edge off negative personality traits while slightly emphasizing positive traits. Similar to using a dimmer switch for a light that's too bright, dialing perfectionism down from ninety to seventy on a one-hundred-point scale can make a huge difference in one's ability to create and sustain strong relationships.

How does this work? Remembering that some traits can be positive at work but negative at home, a client is asked to identify some of their least desirable strong traits where moderation could benefit their relationships, or a few good but weaker traits where enhancement could help. Together the client and counselor identify the origin of these traits along with any ongoing contributing factors that may be exacerbating the trait in question. Long-standing personality characteristics are often being reinforced through material success or other perpetuators. Identifying these can be a useful first step toward generating strategies for change and dialing up or dialing down the traits at issue.

One important thing to remember is that your personality is not the same as your identity. Your identity is how you define yourself in response to the question, "Who am I?" It's a big question and hard to answer. Emotionally and spiritually advanced individuals often see their identity broadly. Such an individual might define himself as "a child of God" or "a member of the human community."

More typically, individuals will define their identity in reference to external factors such as occupation, family heritage, nationality, and the like. For example, the statement "I am an engineer" equates who I am with what I do. This is very common. In our story, Michael was completely invested in the heroic surgeon concept for his self-definition.

If your identity is exclusively tied to your occupation, you may limit your personality development. For example, identifying yourself as an engineer may reinforce being logical, analytical, critical, and a perfectionist. Our character, Michael, couldn't imagine being different, less in control, and more emotional. These seem to threaten his identity as the heroic surgeon.

Your work identity shouldn't be your only identity. In terms of work, you may wear many different hats over your lifetime, so it's better not to get too caught up in identifying with any of them. You are larger than your role. If you can resist narrowly defining yourself, you can be freer to explore different behaviors and to enjoy multiple roles, activities, and behaviors.

Now let's explore the Relationship Ruiners that we listed. If you recognize yourself, don't worry. We've been there too.

EMOTIONAL UNAWARENESS

What are emotions? The shortest and easiest definition is "feelings." It's easy to think that emotions or feelings are just a state of mind, but they are also a "state of body" at the same time. Take a minute to imagine feeling joy, happiness, and contentment. Now try anger, sadness, and frustration. Can you imagine your body full of energy, peaceful, tense, or tired as a result of these? We believe humans are inextricable combinations of mind, body, and spirit. There is only one you with all three parts. Feelings are, therefore, a state of you.

We all have feelings, but despite their universality, emotions can be some of the least understood aspects of our lives. Many individuals have difficulty identifying, experiencing, expressing, and resolving their emotions. This can be especially difficult for Achievers, who may be unemotional, logical, and rational. Partly this may be genetic or natural for them. Or perhaps it came about during their upbringing for one reason or another. On the other hand, some individuals can be too emotional, driven completely by their strong feelings. In the A/C marriage, Connectors are typically more in touch with their own (and even their partner's) emotions than Achievers. Ideally, Achievers and Connectors can learn from each other, appreciate their differences, and work toward common ground in expressing themselves.

Emotions Connect People

We all have feelings. Many times, we keep them hidden from others, afraid to express our sadness, anger, shame, frustration, or similar negative emotions. But this limits our ability to be fully connected to other people. Deep relationships come from shared experiences and feelings, both positive and negative. Healthy relationships allow for the sharing of all feelings, and the more that are shared, the deeper the relationship grows. When you express emotions, others will feel closer to you and understand you better. Share your feelings to connect with others.

Feelings are an essential and unavoidable part of life and are part of what allows us to form lasting relationships, because *emotions connect people*. That strong bond seen among soldiers in the foxhole is an *emotional* bond. Avoiding, denying, suppressing, or simply being unaware of emotions prevent such bonding. Couples that lack emotional connectedness will gradually drift apart to become more like roommates than life partners. Understanding and managing your own feelings is critical to your marriage and any other close relationships you may have or desire.

But many Achievers (and some Connectors) perceive emotions as a weakness that should remain suppressed or at least hidden. Why? Fear. Fear of being rejected, invalidated, or vulnerable powerfully motivates some people to keep feelings bottled up. And fear of internal, psychic pain can lead to individuals denying, ignoring, repressing, or otherwise avoiding their negative emotions, such as sadness. Unfortunately, suppressing negative emotions inadvertently limits positive feelings as well. For example, it's difficult to fully appreciate joy and happiness if you've not experienced, expressed, and resolved feelings of sadness and hurt.

Since feelings connect people, suppressing emotions can result in resentment and detachment from others. Keeping negative feelings inside hinders connections to others and limits relationships. Being open, vulnerable, and able to share feelings helps deepen relationships.

This ability to be aware of your feelings and to express them in the best manner to connect with or influence others is termed "emotional intelligence" or "EQ" (to contrast it with traditional concepts of intelligence and the "intelligence quotient" or "IQ.") Research suggests that EQ is separate from traditional intelligence (IQ) and that it is highly correlated with success in relationships and career.[3, 4] Psychologist Daniel Goleman, author of *Emotional Intelligence,* writes that character and people skills (EQ) are much more important to success in life in general than traditional intelligence measured as IQ.[5] That makes sense when you realize how much you depend on others at home, at the workplace, and elsewhere. How smart you are won't matter if you run roughshod over other people's feelings. Your spouse is much more affected by your awareness of, sensitivity to, and expression of feelings than by your IQ.

Many successful people from all walks of life are intellectual giants but emotional midgets. Almost all couples enter counseling with at least one partner who is lacking in emotional skills, and a majority of the time they could both benefit from improving their emotional intelligence. Research studies bear out the idea that higher emotional intelligence leads to better social and marital relationships.

Needless to say, Michael has low EQ. He's emotionally clueless— unemotional, unaware of feelings, and unable to share the few emotions he actually feels. Jessica describes him as flat or distant in emotional terms. He hasn't had much experience and comfort with his emotions except anger, which is very easy to displace onto others. As a surgeon, he views strong feelings as detrimental, interfering with his ability to focus and maintain composure. Michael feels that nothing good comes from emotions. Jessica is very comfortable sharing her feelings but not so good at managing them, and she isn't that aware of how her sharing affects others. Michael describes her as an emotional roller coaster. At times, she shares too much with Michael, friends, and acquaintances. Also, she has a difficult time letting go of her strong feelings. Sometimes present-day events can cause feelings to well up from twenty years ago.

How Well-Rounded Are You? It is easy in our society to be intellectually overdeveloped while emotionally underdeveloped. Yet in the long term, happiness is more dependent on your EQ than your IQ. Emotional intelligence helps in relationships. Work on identifying your feelings, expressing them, experiencing them, holding on to the positive, and letting go of the negative. Your increasing emotional maturity will lead to greater connectedness. Grow your EQ.

The differences between Michael and Jessica in their approach to emotions are very common in couples but are also very frustrating for both parties. One simple contributor to a couple's inability to express emotions constructively is that many individuals cannot name (or label) how they feel. Use the following self-assessment to consider your own capability in this area.

SELF-ASSESSMENT—EMOTIONAL INTELLIGENCE

How many emotions can you name? Grab a piece of paper and pencil to complete this exercise. Take your time and don't look at the bottom of this page until you are sure that you've listed as many as you can identify. Try for at least twenty.

Think of ways to end this sentence, "I feel _____." Fill in the chart below with your answers.

Well, how did you do? Don't feel too bad if you couldn't come up with twenty. Most people can name less than twelve emotions. Here is a list of sixty-six common emotions that psychologists have identified as distinct from one another:

Emotions

Aggressive	Envious	Miserable
Amused	Excited	Negative
Angry	Exhausted	Nervous
Anxious	Frightened	Nostalgic
Ashamed	Furious	Optimistic

Bashful	Grateful	Overwhelmed
Bored	Greedy	Paranoid
Confident	Guilty	Pressured
Confused	Happy	Prideful
Cranky	Helpless	Relieved
Curious	Hurt	Relaxed
Delighted	Indifferent	Reticent
Depressed	Infatuated	Sad
Disappointed	Innocent	Smug
Disgusted	Insecure	Surly
Ecstatic	Insignificant	Tender
Elated	Kind	Tired
Energetic	Jealous	Undecided
Emotional	Joyful	Violated
Embarrassed	Lazy	Vulnerable
Enraged	Lonely	Wonderful
Enthusiastic	Mellow	Worried

Try this simple exercise to raise your emotional awareness. Pick ten emotions from the list above—five that you see as positive and five that you see as negative—and write them each on an index card. First thing in the morning, shuffle the cards and pick one. That's your emotion for the day. Your job is to identify when you or others around you are experiencing or expressing that emotion. Just identify it. Keep a tally on the card if you wish. At the end of the day, reflect on what you noticed in yourself and others, and share it with your partner. That's it. Sure, it's pretty simple, but do it for a week and you'll be more emotionally aware than you were when you began! You have probably noticed how different people differ with respect to emotion and relationships. Some wear their emotions like the cover of a book. You can see their joy or their sadness in a moment's glance. Others are more reserved and it can be difficult to know how they feel unless they tell you directly. One of your friends has a high degree of empathy, so she understands how you feel in the late afternoon of a stressful workday, while another friend seems clueless to your emotional exhaustion. Connectors are usually more emotionally aware than Achievers.

Achievers are often unaware of their own emotions and frequently don't understand the emotions and emotional needs of others. This is just part of having a low EQ. Achievers often start out in relationships a few steps behind Connectors in emotional development. Consequently, they are often mystified by their Connector partner's tears or other strong feelings and have literally no idea how to respond.

Trying to be helpful, Connectors may make the mistake of identifying their spouse's feelings for them rather than allowing the Achiever to discern his or her own feelings. Instead of improving their closeness it adds to the Achiever's emotional dependency and may cause resentment.

We don't mean to pick on Achievers. We could all stand to increase our EQ or, expressed a different way, to grow in emotional maturity. In fact, for improving your relationships, *the single most important step is to increase your own EQ.*

HYPERACHIEVEMENT DRIVE

To be a top performer in today's business world you almost have to be driven and intense, because these are the kind of people you're competing against for the top jobs. If you're not willing to work longer and harder than the woman in the next cubicle, she gets the promotion and you don't. She's on her way to the corner office, while the top management is saying that you are a good worker but "lack drive." In many respects, business really is a dog-eat-dog environment where only the strongest survive. Overachievement is rewarded, while regular achievement is merely tolerated. Sports, politics, medicine, and law are other areas where strong ambition, drive, and passion for the game help get you to the top. So perhaps you got to the CEO position by being aggressive. Don't expect everyone else to like it. Most people aren't like you. That's why they're not CEOs. However, if you bring this same drive and intensity into your marriage and parenting, it may not go so well.

Many intense top achievers have trouble tolerating delays, mistakes, or incompetence. They have very little patience and want things done yesterday. Time seems critically important. Quick solutions are imperative. Waiting in line for anything is almost unbearable. When something or someone gets in the way, achievers may become irritated, annoyed, or even hostile. Emotions can even explode. And when they do, someone is always hurt. Healthy relationships require time, cooperation, compromise, and compassion, which are often nearly impossible for the naturally driven and intense individual. Here's an example of what we're talking about:

> John was the CEO of a successful medium-sized manufacturing firm and was as intense as they come. He worked ten or more hours a day and surrounded himself with like-minded employees. He was known for telling employees, "If you don't work as hard as I do, do me a favor and join the competition," and he had fired more than one person for his or her "lax attitude about this business."
>
> Unfortunately, John also tried to run his family life like his business. Insistent on "getting things done around here," he was intense and demanding with his wife and two sons about household duties. His wife, Beth, was a full-time mom, which he liked to remind her was not a "real job."
>
> While Beth and his children craved and loving attention from their husband and father, they received frequent unpleasant "performance evaluations" and unwanted

criticism. Even vacations were not relaxing because of John's desire to cram as much as possible into the trip with tightly scheduled events.

Hyperdriven people like John focus on productivity above all else, even in relationships. Stuffing as much goal-oriented activity into a day as possible, driven individuals have a difficult time relaxing, being still, and stopping to smell the roses. On the positive side, they certainly can get a lot accomplished.

> **Are You a "Human Doing" or a Human Being?**
> How easy it is to get caught up in the doing, to do more, and more, and more . . . never stopping to just be. Have you ever slowed down enough to reflect on what's really important to you? Could it be that you've overprioritized achievement? Slow down. Be still. Just be.

But just try living with one of these individuals, especially if you are not cut from the same cloth. They can't slow down. In fact, they may feel tremendous guilt over doing nothing. Most of their activities have a purpose, with goals or objectives (even fun activities), and they focus on the outcome rather than the process. For example, John might like sailing when there is a pre-planned destination or a race in which to compete, but he would never go sailing just to relax and enjoy the wind, water, and sunshine.

Spontaneity, fun, and relaxation are important to relationships, and many Achievers just don't have time for it. Connectors, however, crave this in their relationship with their achieving partner. In fact, Connectors may have a great deal of difficulty understanding why their spouse can't simply relax. In truth, this need for continuous productivity does keep Achievers from emotional attachment with other people, including their spouses. A continuous stream of projects or tasks can keep them disconnected indefinitely, while, paradoxically, they may be of the mind that all this achievement and productivity makes them good providers and parents.

This hyperachievement mentality is fairly common. Dr. Weiss used to work twelve days of every two weeks and tightly scheduled his recreation on his every other weekend off. He felt like he had not accomplished any relaxation if he didn't make it through his list of scheduled activities. (Yes, we know it sounds crazy. It even sounds crazy to him, *now.*)

SELF-ASSESSMENT—HYPERACHIEVEMENT DRIVE

- Are you obsessed with winning, even when it's a board game with your children?
- Do you hate waiting in lines and constantly switch to find the shortest line?
- Do you focus on the outcome of all activities and in the process lose the enjoyment of the journey?
- Is it difficult, if not impossible, for you to sit still and do nothing?
- Do you blow up when someone close to you lacks your intensity and approaches tasks with a laid-back and nonchalant attitude?

What do your answers say about you? Are you willing to ask your spouse for his or her assessment of your drive to achieve? Why or why not?

PERFECTIONISM

Perfectionism is adopting an attitude that only perfect is good enough. If something is less than perfect, it simply doesn't measure up. Sometimes the business world can reinforce this trait, especially in occupations with little tolerance for error where accuracy and precision are top goals; for example, surgeons, pilots, accountants, and air traffic controllers. We might be happy that our accountant or air traffic controller is a perfectionist and a little obsessive-compulsive because it makes him or her better on the job, a job where mistakes have very serious consequences.

But bringing these traits into a relationship is a whole different matter. Trying to achieve and maintain perfection can be draining, time consuming, and counterproductive. People with this trait demand excellence of themselves and others, including their spouse. The perfectionist's expectations are unrealistic, and the demands are draining on both partners.[6, 7]

Decision making is extremely difficult because mistakes are not acceptable. This leads to "paralysis through analysis." It's possible to think too much, to expend too much time and energy seeking the "best" product, service, or solution. Overanalysis becomes incapacitating, preventing any action. The saying "perfect is the enemy of good" captures this trap.

Being so preoccupied with order and details can obscure the major point of activities. For example, a perfectionist planning a family outing to Disney World spent over two hours reviewing the park map to plan the perfect experience for himself and his family. Of course, their day didn't go according to plan. Small children can't and shouldn't be expected to adhere to a rigorous schedule, especially *when they're on vacation*!

Perfectionism can also put a stranglehold on cooperation. For the perfectionist, it's often, "My way or the wrong way." Couples may spend an excessive amount of time and energy arguing over minor issues without being able to compromise. Or the less perfectionistic one (typically the Connector) always gives in. The feelings that emerge can be a great hindrance to intimacy

Michael is a perfectionist. Everything has to be just so or it's not acceptable to him. At the hospital, this is tolerated. He has created exacting procedures for the operating room staff to follow when he is in surgery. His more reasonable requirements specify who will be in the room, what instruments should be available, and how assistance should be given. Clear standards in this area actually help make sure the operation goes well. But he is also insistent on things such as only a certain brand of suture material, a precise room temperature of sixty-five degrees, and having the radio tuned to his favorite classic rock station. As a perfectionist, all of his standards must be met or he becomes irritated and demanding.

At home, Michael expects dinner to be served promptly at seven o'clock p.m., the cars to be parked in exactly the right spots in the driveway, and the house to be orderly and clean at all times. "A place for everything and everything in its place," describes his view of life.

You can imagine how this has gone over with Jessica and the boys through the years. It's not realistic and never was, especially when the boys were younger. Jessica used to work feverishly to have the house in order and dinner on the table for Michael, but it was never perfect. And just like at the hospital, Michael got irritated and demanding. This led to frustration for both Michael and Jessica, leading to anger and resentment.

> Couples may spend an excessive amount of time and energy arguing over minor issues without being able to compromise.

It's no fun to be a perfectionist. Perfectionists are not usually happy inside. For who can be perfect all of the time? Perfectionists often feel like failures. Their never-good-enough mindset matched with a predictably not perfect performance creates fear, guilt, and a sense of unworthiness.

Perhaps you grew up in a family where only perfect was good enough. You might have heard statements like, "If you can't do it right, don't do it at all," and your parents may have focused on your failures and mistakes, constantly pushing you to do better.

If you have this sense that "I am unworthy unless I get things flawless," realize that this is a negative and harmful mindset that you can change. Learning to adjust expectations, set realistic goals, accept mistakes, and appreciate good, not just perfect, can make a huge difference in your relationships and your personal happiness in life.

SELF-ASSESSMENT—PERFECTIONISM

- Do you find it difficult to make a decision about a significant purchase even after you've researched it thoroughly?
- After receiving a generally positive review at work, do you focus on the one negative aspect of the review?
- Do you find it difficult to ask others for help or delegate tasks for fear that they won't do a good job?
- Do you find yourself getting defensive, hurt, or annoyed when your friends or family attempt to give you constructive criticism?

Reflect on your answers. If you're a perfectionist, you probably know it. It's not wrong to be a perfectionist about certain aspects of your life, but attempting and expecting perfection in all areas will only lead to disappointment and frustration for you and others around you, especially your spouse.

CRITICIZING

No one likes to be the subject of negative comments. It's hard to love and be intimate with someone who is always measuring and judging you, especially when that judgment is critical. Nobody hugs porcupines, so . . . don't act like one.

Well, it's hard to stop—isn't it? Have you ever tried? The natural desire to criticize seems to spring from deep inside us. Why is that? There are several basic common denominators in overly critical individuals, which includes perfectionists and analytical types. Examples could include many engineers, physicians, and scientists who routinely need to take an analytical approach to the issues in their respective fields. They must carefully scrutinize situations, weighing all options before proceeding. What's the benefit of this idea? What could go wrong? How could we make it better? What's the absolute worst-case scenario? While this may be the right approach to complex problems, it sometimes tramples the feelings of other people.

Many individuals will interpret the analytical person's approach as criticism. The analyst thinks his fault finding will help create a better solution, but instead he may offend and alienate others. Transferring this analytical approach to the home front will strain relationships, not improve them.

> **Be Partners with Your Spouse**
> The healthiest relationships occur between emotionally healthy people. It's important for each partner to be a "whole person." Neither person should be dependent on the other for completeness. But neither can act completely independently, either. Strive for interdependency. That is, two independent people forging a life together, voluntarily agreeing to work together, trust, and rely on each other. It's hard, but the rewards are worth the effort. Be interdependent, not independent.

Achievers and Connectors can both be critical, but Achievers are more likely to be overly critical of themselves and others. Many Achievers believe that their criticism motivates others and produces better results, which is often not the case. Connectors are more likely to recognize when their critical nature is pushing others away and seek to resolve the hurt feelings.

Some individuals with low self-esteem try to build themselves up internally by putting others down. This may be a defense mechanism to protect them from feeling hurt and rejected. If I reject you before you reject me, then I will feel less pain. In other words, the best defense is a good offense. Criticism can be a way to maintain a protective armor and insulate oneself from anticipated, perceived, or real emotional pain. Unfortunately, this strategy pushes people away and creates alienation and isolation. Here's an example:

Carol and Larry have been married for seventeen years. Carol is a line manager at a specialty circuit board manufacturing company. She is effective at work but is known for her relentless focus on problems, errors, and mistakes as opposed to focusing on what's going well. Her employees are used to her lack of praise and have taken to complimenting each other on their job performance. They bristle at her constant faultfinding, but as a work team, they are able to support each other.

Unfortunately, at home, her husband Larry has become a team of one. Larry works as an in-house accountant for a large hospital and is quite introverted. Friends all say that "Carol wears the pants in the family." Larry is much less assertive than Carol and has never taken issue with her constant criticism. Of course, he doesn't like it, but rather than challenge her, he has withdrawn and has detached emotionally.

Carol and Larry are now in a loveless marriage. Although Carol is the criticizer, it takes two to make a relationship, and Larry's refusal to openly work through this conflict with Carol has also contributed to this negative outcome.

WHO'S IN CHARGE?

Who's in charge of the relationship? In troubled marriages, usually one partner is controlling or attempting to control the other. Sometimes both parties are attempting to control the other one. That's not the relationship we usually envision when we speak of partnership. One partner or the other is not in charge. Partnerships are created by equality, trust, respect, mutual support, compromise, and cooperation.

But a lot of stubborn, hardheaded, and strong-willed people interpret a partnership as: "You doing what I want." None of us wants to be told what to do, but the most acutely control-driven people are especially sensitive to even sharing decision making with

> In sharing our feelings, we allow others to see our "humanness," which draws them closer.

others. This need for control creates conflict in relationships. In fact, our perspective is that the *issue of power and control is at the root of most marital dysfunction.*

Both Achievers and Connectors may vie for control in relationships, but they typically use different means. Connectors tend to be more subtle and creative in their attempts to control their spouses, while Achievers are more direct and overt. Of course there are variations for all personality types, but all attempts to be "in charge" are usually harmful to relationships.

CONCLUSION

Your personality traits are almost certainly part of any relationship problem you're facing. The good news is that change is possible if you have the desire and will to put forth the effort. It takes hard work, but it can be dome. You can learn new skills, change unhelpful thoughts/ attitudes, and replace old behavior with new responses. The first step is becoming aware that change is needed.

THE BOTTOM LINE

- Perfectionism and other personality traits, which may help in the business world, are often harmful in your personal life.
- Emotional intelligence is the key to success in relationships. In sharing our feelings, we allow others to see our "humanness," which draws them closer. In relationships, respond from your heart as well as your head.

- Fear can keep you trapped in old unproductive habits, and courage can help you break free. Paradoxically, once you begin to change, you may wonder why you were so afraid.

Think less, *feel more.*

What Are You Fighting For?

The Paradox of Control

Let's admit it. It's fun to be in charge. We humans seem to have an instinctive need for control. The creation story of Adam and Eve tells of the first couple seeking knowledge in a quest to be powerful and in control. As you recall, things got a lot worse for them as soon as they got what they thought they wanted.

And so it is with us. We are as confused today as they were. Society teaches us that happiness can be found in wealth, power, and success; that being in charge is the way to get things done; and that information is power. The basic message is that by acquiring power and controlling others, we can get things for ourselves and create a good life. But it's just not so.

In relationships, attempting to control your spouse to achieve your imagined perfect relationship creates tension and turmoil that damage that same relationship. It's a paradox, the most important part of which is: The more you try to control the other person, the more likely they will resist change and the less likely you are to get what you want. Conversely, the more you focus on controlling only yourself, the more likely you are to get along with your partner and have the opportunity to build a mutually satisfying relationship.

You can only win the Love Fight *together* with your spouse, not by controlling him or her. Unfortunately, this lesson can be hard to learn.

**The Way to Gain Control
is to Give It Up**

You want your spouse to be this way and your kids to be that way. Good luck with that. It probably won't happen. You can't control others, and the more you try, the more they resist. Conversely, the less you try to control others, the better your relationships will be and the more influence you will have with them. It's a paradox. Attempting to force an outcome often fails, but letting go may help to bring about the desired outcome. Let it happen, rather than make it happen.

Command and control are often highly developed themes for successful people, like Michael, who then become convinced that such power is essential for success. It's counter-intuitive for many to think that you succeed in relationships by not being in control of others.

A physical analogy of this is being caught in a rip current, which is a fast-moving flow of water from the beach out to sea. Even the strongest swimmers are not able to fight the pull of the water. Following their natural instincts and swimming toward shore against the current, many victims tire out and drown. Yet if they were to relax and swim sideways to the shore, they can escape the typically narrow current and then swim to the beach safely.

Sometimes what is intuitive to us might actually be harmful. At the beach, swimmers have to be educated about how to handle themselves in a rip current or they are likely to get it wrong and drown. Similarly, trying to control or change your spouse can seem necessary or essential, but it can drag the relationship under. And just like at the beach, this is often something that must be learned, especially by the strong willed.

Many successful businesspeople, lawyers, doctors, and other professionals are strong willed. They have an inner strength and determination to achieve, despite significant obstacles. Persevering in the face of adversity, delaying gratification to attain a goal, and fighting for a cause despite fierce opposition are common themes for these business and community leaders. Their courage and tenacity is admirable and, after all, it is their strong wills that have equipped them to overcome adversity and achieve their goals. These characteristics have been very positive and helpful in their professional lives. Commonly, strong-willed individuals may also be rigid and stubborn. Having a strong will implies self-discipline and persistence, but it doesn't rule out flexibility. When individuals lose flexibility and aren't open to suggestions or feedback, they become stubborn—someone who doesn't budge an inch and for whom "it's my way or the highway." It's likely that you don't always enjoy being around this person.

No one really likes to be told what to do or how to do it, but these stubborn, hardheaded types resist others' helpful input and advice even when they know they need it. The man at the wheel on the family vacation, lost in unfamiliar territory but unwilling to stop and ask directions or discuss the route with his wife, is a classic example. Achievers often won't ask for or accept help.

Some apply their strong-willed nature to controlling others.[1] But relying on your inner strength to persist through a tough law school curriculum is very different from using it to try to change your spouse. Trying to force anyone to change creates anger, which is followed in short order by resentment and detachment. This isn't just a marital issue; it's a relationship issue. The same successful businesspeople who don't develop close relationships at home don't have many close friends at work either because they are using the same controlling behaviors. Here's an example:

> Tom was accustomed to taking charge at work. Now CEO of a very large firm, he had risen through the ranks to the top spot through determination to be the best. He was proud of his iron will and never backed down from a challenge— personal or professional. The board of directors praised him for the company's financial performance, but his controlling and abrasive style wore on his direct reports. Two vice

presidents had recently resigned and one had been fired for openly disagreeing with Tom.

This may or may not be the best style for a high-powered CEO. Nevertheless, command and control can be effective in the workplace where the focus is on performance, as opposed to loving relationships. Tom demanded respect, not love, from his subordinates. He got that respect, but many employees disliked him.

Tom tried to run his marriage and family as he ran the company. His wife and children might as well have been employees of "Tom, Inc." It was all about him. He decided where to live, what church to join, and where to go on vacation. He alone decided on the amount of the kids' allowance, the model and color of his wife's car, and numerous other matters of family life, both small and large.

Under this tyrannical control, gradually his family relationships deteriorated. Similar to his employees, one of his children had become extremely rebellious, while the other was compliant but highly resentful. His wife reacted in a passive-aggressive fashion, avoiding him through engaging in her own activities. She joined three community service organizations and two tennis teams for the stated purposes of "giving back" and "personal health." What she really wanted was to become too busy to spend time with her husband.

In Tom's case, it wasn't just his relationship with his wife that suffered. He wound up alienating his children, too. This is another common problem for many parents. Of course, in childhood, parents must exert control, but as children grow they must accept progressively more responsibility for their own lives. This requires a corresponding letting go by the parents. Unfortunately, some just won't let go. There are two potential adverse outcomes: the child either gives in to the parents and is less competent, capable, and independent as a result; or he or she rebels and distances himself or herself from the parents. Either way, the parents' goals of having a lasting, loving relationship with their child and raising him or her to become a mature adult are harmed.

SELF-ASSESSMENT—UNDERSTANDING THE HARM OF CONTROL

Consider your own experience with controlling behavior. Imagine the scenarios below and how you felt or would feel: What if:

- Your partner undermines your authority in front of the children?
- The homeowners' association forces you to make repairs or changes to your home that you don't want to make?
- Someone uses their power and authority to get what they want and in the process manipulates you?
- Someone discounts or negates your judgment and makes a decision that affects your life?
- You're forced to be a team player at work and agree with the game plan even when it compromises your morals/values?
- Someone holds you hostage to a mistake you made years ago and will not forgive or let go of his or her anger toward you?
- Someone makes decisions for you without your input?

Could you identify how you would feel in these situations? That's the way most people feel when they experience similar treatment.

CONTROLLING OTHERS—WHY DO WE TRY?

If controlling behavior is so harmful to relationships, why is it so common? Spouses try to control each other. Parents try to control adolescent or even adult children. Bosses try to control workers. Yes, controlling behavior is everywhere. Why *is* that?

Much of this is due to *fear and insecurity*. When individuals struggle with fear or insecurity, a natural tendency is to seek control over their environment and the people in their lives. This type of fear is not your ordinary day-to-day understandable fear, like fear of the vicious dog that lives next door. It is an underlying, deep-rooted insecurity or anxiety that is part of many people's personality. Here are some common fears:

- *I'm a fraud.*
- *Everyone thinks I'm great but I'm really not.*
- *If they knew the real me they wouldn't like me.*
- *I will never be accepted.*
- *No one can love me.*
- *I don't measure up.*
- *Someday the truth will come out and I'll have no friends.*
- *I can't let anyone see the real me.*
- *If I don't please him/her, he/she will leave.*
- *I'm a failure.*
- *I've got everyone fooled; at least I hope I do.*
- *I don't deserve love.*
- *If I died today, no one would attend my funeral.*

These fears or insecurities may or may not be realistic. You might really be a fraud, accepting the "star performer" award from your boss after stealing credit for another person's work. But for most of us, these thoughts are simply not true. An internal critique of our outwardly acceptable job performance gets magnified and distorted in our minds to become the thought that "I'm a fraud." These fears are often lurking just below the conscious level, but they're always active and can drive a lot of controlling behaviors.

For individuals with strong fear, controlling behaviors are a protective response. Through controlling and achievement, they are able to suppress the fear and assure themselves that they are successful and therefore valued. Often their mental model is that achievement and success are necessary in order to be acceptable, lovable, and to receive love. You could express it this way, "I'm appreciated for what I accomplish, not for who I am."

So control is essentially an instinctual way to manage these fears. For some people, exposure to an uncontrollable environment may create a sense of helplessness contributing to depression.[2] You can consider it to be a version of the "fight" in the fight-or-flight response. Ordinary stress and fear can trigger our body's primitive survival response just as well as a real life-threatening event, and our reaction to fear is often to try to exert control.

Imagine yourself riding in the front passenger's seat of a car, perhaps teaching your child to drive, when you get worried that your child is braking too slowly to avoid ramming into the car in front of you. Can you picture yourself tensing your body and braking hard with your right foot automatically even though you are not driving? Would you appeal to your child in an attempt to control how he is braking, only to have him assure you that he is aware and in control of the situation?

Sometimes growing up with extremely controlling parents causes a young adult to vow never to be controlled again. The intense feelings of helplessness, powerlessness, anger, resentment, and fear experienced in childhood produce a need in her to always be in charge. You can think of it as an "I'll control you so you don't control me" response.

Fear is the common denominator of all this controlling, and naturally, those affected aren't able to relinquish control and be vulnerable. *What if*

> **The Opposite of Fear Is Trust**
> Fear feels bad. Very bad. In an effort to avoid the outcome we fear, we try to control things and people. Often this makes things worse and our fears increase. These fears keep us stuck, preventing us from living life fully. Strive to live free from fear.

things go wrong? What if my kids don't pass the course? What if my business fails? Then everyone would know that I'm a failure. In seeking to control others, these individuals are seeking to suppress, deny, or refute their fears. They may also equate failure with inadequacy and incompetence when, in fact, growth often occurs through failure and defeat.

Are these kinds of thoughts realistic? Are you truly a failure as a person if your children don't pass the course? Are you really a fake or a fraud because there are some minor flaws in your work that go unrecognized by others? No, these kind of thoughts are not realistic, but they are very common. You have probably experienced them or something similar yourself. It can be helpful to think of fear as an acronym for False Evidence Appearing Real. We can spend a lot of time and energy defending against imagined disasters with a variety of controlling behaviors. These overprotective, and unnecessary, responses can take a toll on our relationships. Learning to let go of the fear allows us to also let go of the unproductive controlling response.

The interesting part is that it's often the *most* successful individuals from society's standpoint who harbor the most fear. In trying to suppress the fear, they have been driven to control and achieve far beyond the norm. However, no accomplishment can fully release them from their unrealistic fears. It's as if they're running faster and faster to get somewhere, not realizing that they're on a treadmill. Most high achievers don't understand that their actions aren't helping, because their desired destination is off the treadmill.

Those on the fear/control/achievement treadmill may not get where they want, but they do get somewhere. Often it's to a crisis. Their drive toward control and achievement harms their relationships. In the end, no amount of material possessions and worldly success will compensate for a lack of attention to relationships. Relationships take time, energy, and flexibility that these people seemingly don't have. But "presents" are no substitute for "presence."

Trapped on their fear/control/achieve treadmill, these individuals are unlikely to voluntarily seek therapy. A Connector spouse will often seek individual counseling about a relationship with a very controlling Achiever. As the Connector begins to change—becoming more assertive, saying no more often, and setting better boundaries—the Achiever may be pushed out of his or her comfort zone. It's typical that when one partner is growing and changing, the relationship comes under pressure and the other partner will respond. In the best cases, the Achiever spouse also chooses to grow emotionally, perhaps through therapy, and the relationship is strengthened. But sometimes the Achiever may respond more negatively and the relationship is further threatened.

This is what we meant when we said earlier that the more you try to control the other person, the less likely you are to get what you want; and the more you focus on controlling only yourself, the more likely you and your partner will have a mutually satisfying relationship. Saying it another way, when you try to control your partner, you force her to stand her ground. When you focus on changing yourself, you give her the freedom to choose to change, or not. As you grow in emotional maturity, she is likely to grow and change too. But even if not, you are better prepared emotionally to manage what comes.

SELF-ASSESSMENT—AM I CONTROLLING?

Do you:

- Always have to drive the car?
- Find it difficult to ask for or accept help?
- Find it difficult to delegate tasks because you would rather do it yourself?
- Have a difficult time sharing your feelings and trusting that others won't use them against you?
- Have a hard time admitting when you're wrong?
- Prefer making your decisions without the input of others?

It's easy to be controlling without recognizing it. If you see yourself here, don't look to justify your answers. Just accept them. It's okay to own up to these traits, as long as you are willing to work on them.

FORMS OF CONTROL

What does control look like? You might have the image of a drill sergeant barking orders or a CEO giving direction to her subordinates. It can be that blatant in marriage and family relationships, too, but it can also appear in other, more subtle but damaging forms.

What reactions do these words bring to mind: coercion, emotional abuse, physical abuse, manipulation, criticizing, intimidation, nagging, whining, threats, persuasion, passive-aggressiveness, and withholding? All of them are techniques used in an attempt to control others.

MANIPULATION

Manipulation is a form of control where things are managed deviously or behind the scenes. If you are being manipulated, you might not be aware of it. Car salesmen are legendary for manipulating the sales process to get you to pay a higher price for your new ride. Some businesspeople are masters of arranging allies, setting up circumstances, and presenting facts in just the right ways to convince you of their merit. Many may bring this type of control into their family relationships, too. Frequent use of manipulation will eventually be uncovered, leading to mistrust and resentment.

One example of manipulation is guilt tripping. By inducing guilt in the other person, we can try to get them to do what we want. Statements like, "If you really loved me, you would _____" or "You are only concerned about yourself, otherwise you would _____" are typical of this approach. The blanks we've left might be filled in with examples like these:

- have sex with me more
- buy me a new car
- stand up for me (even if I was wrong)
- work less and spend more time with me
- keep the house clean and neat

Now, it may be that the need for a new car is a legitimate issue meriting discussion, but the framing is designed to win, not to discuss, negotiate, and reach an agreement. A person who is prone to guilt or self-doubt may be powerfully affected by comments like these. Not having enough self-worth to see through the criticism, they may give in without expressing their view and negotiating the matter in order to receive acceptance from the manipulator.

> Frequent use of manipulation will eventually be uncovered, leading to mistrust and resentment.

Laura was a master manipulator, working behind the scenes to make sure things went her way without it being apparent that she was behind it all. Her approach to family vacations illustrates this. Laura preferred traveling to the mountains while her husband, Charlie, liked the beach. Knowing that Charlie hated to disappoint the kids, she would carefully sow her ideas for the annual family vacation in the minds of her two young children well in advance.

Laura then ensured that the kids were involved in any conversation with Charlie about vacation plans, and she justified this by insisting that "vacations are about children" and "they're old enough to have a vote." When it came time to finally decide on a destination and plan the trip, the children always voted to travel where she had wanted to go all along. Not once in their eleven-year marriage had the family ever vacationed at any of Charlie's favorite spots.

That's just one example. Laura took a similar approach to decisions regarding what restaurants to frequent, which movies to see, and even who Charlie should have for personal friends. Eventually Charlie wised up to this technique. Over time, he began to realize how fully Laura had taken control of their relationship through manipulation. He felt betrayed and very angry. As a result of marriage counseling, today they have a strong, loving relationship.

In counseling, Charlie worked through his resentment and learned to be more assertive. Laura learned to be less manipulative and to deal with conflicts directly. They both learned to negotiate and compromise when making decisions, to prioritize their relationship, and to be a team when it came to raising the children.

WITHHOLDING

Withholding is not so devious but just as damaging, and can be considered a special form of passive-aggressiveness. Essentially it's a way of punishing another person by keeping, or withholding, something from them in an attempt to make them change. Withholders are basically saying to their spouse, "If you want what I've got, you have to do as I say." It's the adult version of the childhood spat that ends when one kid says, "Oh yeah? Then I'm taking my ball and going home!"

Common examples are the withholding of money, love, sex, forgiveness, time, and even conversation or communication in troubled relationships. A stereotypical example of this behavior is a husband refusing to give money to his wife, and the wife who won't sleep with her husband. Of course, it happens the other way around as well. Once again, this type of controlling behavior *never* works over the long term and *always* creates anger and resentment.

Scott and Sara were both withholders. Scott took issue with Sara's spending too much time and energy on tennis and socializing with her friends at the courts. He dealt with this by giving her the silent treatment, often going for three or four days without speaking to her, acting as if she didn't exist. Sometimes Sara would cut back her tennis and socializing for a few weeks just to get Scott to speak to her again. Of course, this didn't help in the long run. In fact, it fostered resentment, but Scott had never learned to talk things out.

Sara had issues with Scott, too. She resented his long hours at work and his driven nature. She often felt that he put work first and the family second. Truth is—he did. Imitating Scott, she also used withholding, including withholding sex, with the intention of changing his behaviors. And again, it worked in the short run. Scott would be home early when his desire for sex reached a peak every few weeks, but he was beginning to talk with an admiring female coworker about how "my wife doesn't understand me."

Both Scott and Sara are placing their marriage at risk and each will likely blame the other when the crisis finally breaks.

PASSIVE-AGGRESSIVENESS

Passive-aggressiveness seems to be a contradiction in terms. Combining aggression (the active attempt to control a person or situation) with what looks to be passivity (inactivity or submissiveness), passive-aggressive individuals resist partnering and attempt control in relationships by indirect means. Passive-aggressive techniques include avoidance, procrastination, sullenness, and feigned incompetence or sabotage. The person

Passive-Aggressiveness: Control without Conflict

Have you ever worked with someone who said yes but meant no? They promised a lot but found excuses to deliver a little? How long did it take for you to figure out their passive-aggressive style was a means of getting what they wanted? This is how a passive-aggressive person "wins" while avoiding conflict. It's sneaky. It's not honest, not genuine. Being indirect, covert, and vindictive are hallmarks of passive-aggressiveness. These folks smile to your face while secretly undermining you. True resolution of conflict requires direct communication. Be open. Say what you mean and mean what you say.

might agree to a course of action but then procrastinate until it's too late, or perform their part so badly that they are excused from doing it again.

You can think of this covert and indirect action as being similar to guerrilla warfare. In warfare, guerrilla attacks are against targets of opportunity, unpredictable, and not directly related to any particular action by the other side. In a marriage, it might play out this way:

Helen is very upset over an offhand comment by her husband, Bob, but says nothing to him at the time. The next day she is still miffed at Bob, and she's looking for revenge. Bob's friend Mike calls to invite Bob fishing the day after tomorrow, but Bob's out when Helen answers the phone. She agrees to take a message while having absolutely no intention of passing it on to Bob.

Three days later, after missing the fishing trip, Bob gets a call from Mike wondering why he never responded to the invitation. Now Bob's angry and confronts Helen, who meekly replies that she "forgot." Of course it wasn't about forgetting, it was about getting even.

One obvious problem with this approach is that Bob never finds out what Helen was upset about. How can he change? How can Helen ever expect things to be different? Or often, when the true issue comes to light, the parties blow up in long-suppressed anger. Again, there is no opportunity for correction, growth, or change.

Some people are unaware of their frequent use of passive-aggressive behavior. Perhaps they were raised in an environment where anger was not allowed or punished and learned to suppress and deny these feelings. Passive-aggressiveness may have become a safe way to release their strong emotions. Of course, it's not a good way.

Here's another example:

> Larry couldn't handle conflict and avoided it at all cost. Instead, he would agree to accommodate others while internally becoming angry, resentful, and determined to get his way. Larry often said yes while meaning no. His usual ploy was incompetence.
>
> He was annoyed when his wife, Melissa, asked him to help with housecleaning and laundry while she would be away on a two-day business trip. Larry begrudgingly agreed to help, and then he purposely mixed colors with whites, ruining several of Melissa's favorite outfits. When confronted upon her return, Larry claimed that he didn't know that the two couldn't be mixed together. Melissa never asked him to do laundry again.

EMOTIONAL AND PHYSICAL ABUSE

Worse than passive-aggression is outright aggression in the form of emotional and/or physical abuse.

Emotional abuse is a pattern of belittling or putting down someone verbally. *You're so stupid. You can't do anything right. You're lucky to have me because no one else would want you. You could never survive on your own.* These are some common abusive put-downs. Often not healthy emotionally in the first place, the victim of emotional abuse finds himself or herself walking on eggshells trying to avoid the abuse. Living in constant fear, he or she gradually becomes more submissive and dependent on the abuser as the threats, belittling, humiliation, and rejection take their toll on his or her spirit.

In many cases, victims of verbal or emotional abuse have heard these put-downs before, maybe from their parents, siblings, peers, or even coaches/mentors. People get used to and tend to accept what is familiar to them, even if it's unhealthy and inappropriate.

Constant criticism wears people down. Even mild habitual criticism can be a form of control, which harms relationships. Do any of these sound familiar? *You're not going to wear that, are you? You embarrass me when _____. I know you can do better than that. What will others think of you when _____? You're not planning to do that, are you? What are you thinking?* The ultimate goal of these statements is to influence you to behave the way the speaker wishes.

Emotional abuse often works. People are controlled, but at what cost? Some individuals may even convince themselves that they deserve this type of relationship or that they could never attract better treatment. Psychologically, they are often simply incapable of leaving. This distorted thinking is part of what keeps people stuck in dysfunctional relationships.

Gradually, this verbal and emotional bullying may lead to physical bullying and intimidation. Or physical abuse may predominate over emotional abuse. Threats of physical harm are very coercive. And when such threats are made, they should be taken seriously. Punching, kicking, choking, and other forms of physical violence are the ultimate weapons of controlling behavior in relationships. This is more common than most people recognize. Violence in relationships is reported by 31 percent of married women.[3] This is not just a women's issue. Over 25 percent of men report having experienced physical abuse from an intimate partner.[4]

The abused spouse may feel completely trapped, and the warning—*If you leave, I will kill you*—is too often true.

SPECIAL NOTE ON ABUSE

If you are in a physically abusive relationship, *you must get out. The abuse, control, and violence will get worse. Do not threaten to leave or negotiate with the abuser.* It is *vital* that you not let the abuser know of your desire or plans to leave. Instead, you should seek help from others and make your plans in secret. The best resource is often a Domestic Abuse Hotline, which can be found in the Emergency Numbers section of your local telephone directory. Other appropriate actions would be to confide in your doctor or your clergyperson, who will likely know how to connect you with other resources to leave safely.

> The dysfunctional parent-child pattern is a recipe for resentment, hurt, and disconnectedness.

In an abusive situation, nothing is more important than the physical well-being of you and your children. Your safety and the safety of your children are more important than the relationship, the abuser, your job, or your future. Once you and they are safe, you can deal with other issues with people who can support you. *Concern yourself with only one thing— how to leave safely.*

CARETAKING

Physical violence and intimidation are the ultimate means of control, in that they render the other party helpless and powerless. An opposite method for rendering someone helpless and powerless is caretaking, which may be the least recognized control situation.

In short, caretaking is doing for another person what they could and should do for themselves. It looks helpful, loving, and kind, but in reality, it's just another form of control. Through his or her actions, the caretaker creates an unnecessary, artificial, dependent relationship with another person.

Here's how it works. Typically, acting out of concern, the caretaker attempts to fix, solve, or otherwise take care of problems or issues for another, without allowing that person much involvement or control. Quickly the caretaker can become responsible for many aspects of the other person's life. The cared-for individual becomes more passive, assuming little responsibility for himself or herself. In the process of being taken care of, this person has come under the control of the caretaker.

In today's society, excessive caretaking may be most often recognized in parent-child relationships. Young children need a lot of care and guidance, but as children grow up, they gradually need to accept increasing responsibility for their own lives. Many parents are overprotective, sheltering their kids from mistakes and failures. In so doing, they help to create dependency, insecurity, and low self-esteem in their children, who might find themselves unprepared for an independent life as young adults.

Here are several examples from marriages that you might recognize:

> Howard and Jean have been married for thirty-five years. During that time, Howard has managed their financial life. He has paid all the bills, opened the bank accounts, negotiated for new cars and other major purchases, made the investments, and decided on all significant financial matters. Jean is fine with all of this. As she explains it, "I just don't have a head for money and finances."

> Bob and Alice have been together for nearly fifty years, after growing up in the same small town as children. Over the last twenty years Bob has become a technophile and adapted better than most to the information age. But Alice has never learned to use a computer or smartphone. *"I leave that to Bob,"* she says. *"Computers are so complicated, and I just*

don't have a head for electronics." Bob maintains all the online business and personal relationships for the couple.

Roberta and Joe have been through a lot in their two decades of married life, including serious illness. Joe has several chronic but stable medical conditions, including diabetes, and sees multiple doctors. Roberta attends to all of Joe's medical appointments and responds to any of the doctor's questions to Joe. *"Well, doctor, his blood sugar has been fine and he feels good."* When pressed to answer for himself, Joe is unable to say how he's doing and usually defers to his wife.

We can call this situation a "parent-child marriage" because of the inappropriate, unequal roles the spouses have assumed. In an actual parent-child relationship, the parent must have more responsibility and authority because the child is not yet an adult. However, in marriage the partners should assume responsibility for their own lives as individuals with joint responsibility for the relationship.

Other examples might be:

- A controlling, belittling, aggressive husband (parent) with a detached and disrespectful wife (child)
- A nagging, scolding, and demanding wife (parent) with a defiant, rebellious, and immature husband (child)

CARETAKING-PARENT-CHILD RELATIONSHIPS

Parent-child elements are present in our story of Michael and Jessica. Jessica assumed responsibility for Michael's emotions, social relationships, and connections since "he didn't get that sort of thing." Michael was allowed to avoid responsibility for interpersonal relationships; he didn't share in the emotional burden of the family. Jessica told him what he should be feeling and did the emoting for the family. Over time, this didn't

> **"Changing" Others Is a Way to Avoid Changing Yourself**
>
> "He needs to change." "She needs to work on herself." It's easier to focus on the other person's issues. Maybe you're even right, but that's not the point. What is the point? Two things: One, focusing on others is mainly a way to divert your focus from yourself, and two, you can't change anyone else anyway. Focus on what you can control—yourself. Change yourself, and see how others respond.

work out as well as both might have hoped. Both Michael and Jessica were unhappy with their roles but became stuck in the destructive pattern and didn't know how to change.

This inappropriate parent-child phenomenon is quite common in marriage and other relationships. Often partners may alternate roles of parent or child in various aspects of the relationship. For instance, Michael assumed the parent role when it came to money and financial matters, even as he was the child in emotional and relational matters. In this dynamic, the parent tends to be domineering, condescending, and controlling, while the child is often impulsive, immature, and passive-aggressive.

Imagine being married to one of your actual parents or children. The dysfunctional parent-child pattern is a recipe for resentment, hurt, and disconnectedness. Sometimes this dysfunctional dynamic can be much more subtle and hard to recognize. However, because of the complementary nature of the dynamic, it may even feel good at first.

For example, a common scenario includes an extroverted, talkative, and emotional person paired with an analytical, reserved, and socially awkward person. They complement each other beautifully. They feel fine about their combined strengths and weaknesses. Ideally, they would take on nurturing, encouraging, and supportive roles with one another, enabling further healthy, joint evolution and development of any parts of the self that may be childlike, immature, or underdeveloped. Often, however, the partners each begin to reinforce the other's weaknesses and create feelings of resentment. Then an unequal parent-child relationship has taken hold and may be difficult to break until there's a crisis.

If Michael and Jessica are to break out of their parent-child relationship, each will need to clearly identify how their "adult" role is different from what they're doing now and implement strategies to change. And change is rarely easy. Adults communicate assertively and deal with conflict directly. Other adult behaviors include avoiding blame and defensiveness, while taking responsibility for their own actions and words. Adults are able to apologize, forgive, and let go of negative emotions without harboring a grudge. Adults can also learn new skills and initiate behaviors without having to be prodded or pressured. Two adults can maintain a healthy marriage much easier than partners who tend to fulfill the roles of parent and child.

To have an adult-adult relationship, both parties must take full responsibility for their own lives, thoughts, actions, and emotions.

CARETAKING-CODEPENDENCY

A specialized instance of caretaking behavior can be seen in codependency with enabling. The term "codependency" is typically used to describe when the partner of a person addicted to alcohol, drugs, or destructive behavior is psychologically dependent on that person. The partner is then said to be codependent. The codependent partner will then often engage in enabling, which means taking actions that help (or enable) the addicted person to continue their unproductive behavior. Because these terms are gaining some popular use outside of addiction, you may hear them applied to more ordinary situations.

But remember, even where caretaking is not intentionally about control, *enabling is disabling*. The more we do for others what they could and should do for themselves, the more we help to produce dependence and a feeling of inadequacy in them. This applies to many aspects of life. Perhaps you really are better at managing the finances, communicating/

listening, sharing emotion, developing friendships, or some other aspect of life than your spouse. That doesn't mean you should be in charge of that area all the time. Your spouse can participate, learn, and grow in your areas of strength just as you can in his or hers.

We must allow our partners and others to assume responsibility for their own lives. There is no better expression of this than the old Chinese proverb, "Give a man a fish and you feed him for a day. Teach a man to fish and you feed him for a lifetime." Stop handing out fish.

Excessive caretaking does a disservice to both parties and keeps people dependent on each other. Although caretaking might be well intentioned, the underlying message conveyed could be, "I don't think you're capable of handling this situation, so I'll assume responsibility for you, and by doing so, I'll be able to control what and how we do things."

BEING CONTROLLED BY OTHERS

The flip side of controlling others is being controlled by others. As the expression goes, "It takes two to tango." If one is controlling, the other must be somehow allowing it or permitting it to continue. People don't make a conscious decision, "I'm going to let myself be controlled in my relationship," but rather that some combination of fear, insecurity, and apparent lack of options keeps them stuck in a disagreeable situation. Most people who are being controlled want to be able to create, choose, and have the emotional strength to act on new options.

> Most people who are being controlled want to be able to create, choose, and have the emotional strength to act on new options.

Perhaps when reading the description of a controller you said to yourself, "That's my spouse!" If so, your spouse is controlling or attempting to control you. How did you get a spouse like that? Or, why have the two of you allowed this to happen? Typically, individuals on this side of the relationship also have a reason for their behavior. In other words, they get something from allowing themselves to be controlled. Similar to the dominant partner, they often also have fears or insecurities that are assuaged by remaining in this less-than-optimal situation. Low self-esteem often plays a major role. Here are some typical thoughts people in this situation may experience. *I couldn't make it on my own. She's right; no one else would want me. I'm lucky to have what I have. If she leaves, I will be lost. How will I survive without her?*

You can see how thinking like that allows the relationship to continue unchanged. It's the same in the world of work. Many people feel stifled at their present job, yearn for something different, and yet remain trapped in their position by fear. *What if I can't make the same salary? What if I had to move? What would people think about me?* The fear keeps them trapped.

If we don't take action, nothing will change. Action requires courage, faith in self, and a game plan to give you hope for the future. Taking control of our lives might mean getting a job (or a different job), starting an exercise program, taking an assertiveness class, receiving counseling, joining a support group, attending church, or incorporating positive self-statements. After you've accepted and acknowledged what the problem is, the next step is to seek solutions and strategies to modify your approach, attitude, and actions. Finally, the implementation phase requires determination and perseverance. As the Nike slogan goes, "Just do it."

In an ideal marriage, neither partner is controlling or being controlled. And each partner assumes responsibility for his or her own thinking and behavior. So if you are the one being controlled, recognize that you must also work to overcome your fear, identify new options, and change your own behavior to set yourself free. Strive to change yourself first.

THE BOTTOM LINE:

- Trying to control situations, events, and people is instinctive but harmful, and controlling behavior is typically the major problem in troubled marriages.
- Paradoxically, relinquishing control often leads to having more influence. In a committed relationship, the more freedom each partner gives the other, the stronger the bond.
- Once again, fear is the biggest obstacle to seeing this. This is the human condition. We are all fearful or insecure about something, but we can get past our fears to learn and grow.

Controlling behavior *kills marriages.*

History Is Not Destiny

Leaving Your Past Behind

Most people have limited insight into the continuing influence of their past experiences. But as Wordsworth wrote, "The child is father of the man."

When it comes to raising kids, it's common for parents to overcompensate for their own suboptimal childhood environment. In trying too hard at providing for their children, they may wind up handing down new dysfunctional behavior patterns. Personality development is not completely understood and is certainly multifactorial. Psychologists and other experts disagree on the desirability and necessity of understanding "how I got this way" when you're trying to focus on "how to be different." Our main message in this book is that you *can* take action to be different and improve your relationships. Sometimes people choose to fixate on the past, causing them to remain stuck and consumed by negative emotion. But understanding your past and its impact on your present can help you to change your future. You have a choice: you can fixate on the problems of the past and remain stuck, or you can take responsibility for changing and be set free. Wouldn't you prefer to have explanations rather than excuses?

CHILDHOOD

We spend our whole childhood growing. We grow physically, emotionally, and mentally. Our parents' job is to help us. The main goal of childrearing should be to help the child learn and grow into a mature, capable adult. In the ideal environment, a child is given unconditional love and encouragement. She is allowed to try new things, to succeed, and to fail in a supportive environment. She is valued for who she is, not for what she does or accomplishes. Her parents model mature adult behaviors, and she learns by firsthand experience and observation. When she misbehaves, she is corrected promptly and receives nonabusive, proportionate discipline.

> Everyone has at least some emotional issues, fears, or insecurities in at least one area of life.

However, the truth is that most people don't grow up in an environment like that. Almost everybody is raised in a household with at least some unhealthy parenting, trauma, or conflict. And so we all develop some issues, or dysfunctional personality traits. Often these issues arise because they are adaptive or make sense while being raised in a less-than-perfect childhood home. These same traits are usually maladaptive or harmful when manifested in our lives as adults.

Everyone has at least some emotional issues, fears, or insecurities in at least one area of life. These can lead to behavior that can harm relationships, but you can work through them and grow in emotional health.

So, what was your home life like? How did your parents deal with conflict? How did you deal with stress and conflict as a child? How well did your parents communicate? What was your role in your family? Answering these kinds of questions can help you determine what impact your childhood may have had on your development and subsequent behavior as an adult.

Perhaps you were the oldest child and were pushed to take charge, to be responsible for everyone. Or perhaps you were the rebellious child.

Rebellious children may misbehave or act out to lessen parental conflict by shifting the focus onto themselves. Or they may simply be seeking attention from their parents. Even negative attention can seem better than no attention. Some children deal with stress through avoidance and detachment—others through confrontation and acting out. Are you, perhaps inadvertently, using these roles and reactions from your childhood in your adult relationships today?

Several childhood themes are common among Achievers, including loss, emotional abuse, conditional love, and parental enabling of irresponsibility. Often, through therapy, these business-winners/relationship-losers come to see their childhood experiences as being directly linked to their business success and their relationship difficulties. Connectors may have had some of the same childhood experiences, but instead of coping through achievement they focus on building relationships.

Loss

Two major forms of loss in childhood are the death of a parent or the parents' divorce. Both can be devastating to the child who doesn't understand or accept what happened or why. Death and divorce frequently produce overwhelming grief, fear, and helplessness. The child may blame herself, but even if she doesn't, she will often still develop fear of loss in the future. Or she may interpret the events as abandonment or rejection. And the surviving parent or the divorcing couple may be too caught up in their own needs to help the child successfully navigate through this emotional minefield.[1, 2]

If the child is not helped to understand what's occurring, accept and express her feelings, and resolve these emotions in a healthy manner, she may find other ways to avoid or suppress them. She might focus on taking action and productivity as a means of distraction from sadness. All of this action may make her appear to be successful and produce rewards that are more under her control than are life, death, and divorce.

Trust and commitment in relationships are problematic for her because a similar loss might happen again. The thinking (perhaps even below conscious awareness) might be: *I trusted my parents and look what happened. I can only trust myself and what I do have control of.* The illusion of control over things and people creates a lot of frustration, angst, and resentment. Life becomes about attaining material wealth, since things appear to be safer and easier to manage than people.

> The illusion of control over things and people creates a lot of frustration, angst, and resentment.

So the unprocessed emotions from the loss result in an excessive drive to achieve. This might be manifested in many different areas—business, academics, diet and exercise, volunteerism, etc. Achieving in these areas is a good thing, but even positive or productive behaviors can be harmful if they are taken to the extreme, which is usually the case if they are used as a means to avoid dealing with the emotions linked to loss. Here's an example in an adult:

> Following a divorce, Elizabeth, the sole proprietor of a gift basket business, immerses herself in her work. She spends more than ten hours a day, six or seven days a week, on the business for months. By focusing her energy on the tangible holiday baskets she produces, she avoids dealing with her intangible and painful emotions. Ironically, she works hardest at the holidays when her feelings of loss and sadness threaten to surface. Over time, she becomes increasingly isolated from friends and family and experiences a great deal of loneliness.

Dr. Ferretti had the following experience with loss:

> My mother died when I was thirteen. Reacting to that, I directed my energy toward achievement and accomplishment as a means of avoiding emotional pain, controlling life, and

securing my father's approval. Over time my drive to achieve only intensified and my competitiveness grew. This need for control and approval, combined with a desire to help others work through their losses, led me to a bachelor's, master's, and PhD in psychology.

However, my emotional immaturity almost caused me to blow my own chance for a happy marriage to my wife, Allison. We had been dating for two years when it was right for my career to move to a distant city. It was clear that it was time to get married or separate. Although I loved Allison, my fear of commitment caused me to behave in ways designed to break up the relationship.

I don't think I really understood what I risked losing. Fortunately, as I faced the impending breakup, several wise friends and mentors helped me recognize and face this fear of commitment that had resulted from my own loss. I was able to shift my thinking, grow emotionally, and choose to marry Allison.

SELF-ASSESSMENT—LOSS

Has a childhood loss affected you?

- Is it difficult to trust others and let people get close?
- Do you rely exclusively on yourself and rarely ask for help from others?
- Is it difficult to be vulnerable in relationships and self-disclose?
- Do you find yourself rejecting others before being rejected?
- Do you always have a backup relationship in development before ending your current one?

Reflect on your answers. Are you afraid of more losses to come? Is that realistic or appropriate now? Is it helping you?

EMOTIONAL ABUSE

Some children are raised in emotionally abusive environments. They grow up with hypercritical and judgmental parents, from whom they hear things like this: *You're so stupid. You'll never amount to anything. Your sister is much better than you'll ever be.* Or they hear milder but still critical statements like: *You could've done better. Less than perfect is not good enough.*

Repeatedly hearing these negative assessments can lead to distorted thinking in a child who accepts these false statements at face value and incorporates them into her own thought processes. In other words, the child takes over where her parents left off! By the time she is an adult, these thoughts are ingrained into her basic consciousness and can drive a lot of unproductive behavior.[3]

> Sue grew up hearing: "You're so stupid. You'll never amount to anything. Your sister is much better than you'll ever be." Because of this, Sue was driven to achieve straight As in college and law school. After graduation, she joined a prestigious law firm in New York and made partner in record time, placing severe physical and emotional stress on herself in the process. She had a strong need to prove her worthiness as a human being in order to secure love and acceptance. It was only after her collapse from exhaustion that she realized that her work drive and ambition were a defensive reaction to her parents' criticism. She had been subconsciously trying to prove them wrong. Over eight months of therapy, she came to see that she had nothing to prove to anyone and was freed of her seeming addiction to work.

Essentially, Sue had been seeking external affirmation because she wasn't able to generate self-esteem. Lacking parental support, encouragement, and approval as a child had helped to create a negative self-image that she fought against through achievement. This is very common. In therapy, Sue came to value herself for herself, independent of any accomplishment. She continued to be a hard worker and was motivated to achieve, but she was no longer driven to do so.

Other forms of emotional injury or abuse may be subtler. Parents may be emotionally labile, volatile, or unpredictable so that the rules aren't clear to the children. The kids aren't sure from minute to minute if they will be praised and embraced or hollered at. Or there may be a lack of emotion, especially love. Some parents never kiss, hug, praise,

> Our feelings can significantly influence and motivate our behaviors. Our goal should be to experience and manage them well so our present behavior is not controlled by past experiences.

or even acknowledge their children in a positive way. These parents and their children have difficulties with emotional attachment and connection. They may find it difficult to trust others and allow themselves to be vulnerable in relationships.

Physical abuse, such as whippings or beatings, is at the other end of the severity scale. Typically physical abuse occurs as part of a larger emotionally abusive environment and compounds the adverse effects on the children.[4] Long-lasting physical and emotional damage may result. Although physical bruises and broken bones may heal with time, emotional bruises may persist and result in long-term emotional harm.[5] Growing up in any form of emotionally abusive environment can create obstacles to the child's ability to understand and express his own feelings. It may not have been safe to do so. He might be risking more abuse from his parents if he were to reveal his anger, pride, sadness, or other emotions. Of course, when your emotional expression is punished, squelched, denied, or invalidated, you learn that you should keep everything to yourself. Many people simply didn't have good emotional role models in their parents. Some parents just aren't that good at helping their kids develop emotionally and may even be a little cold toward them. The phrase "children should be seen and not heard" embodies this approach. You wouldn't expect a child to learn English from parents who only speak French. The same is true of emotional development and expression.

How exactly this plays out in adulthood is highly variable and depends on the nature and severity of the childhood environment, the child's innate resilience, and any support system that may be present (such as friends and other relatives who love and support the child). As a coping mechanism, many learn to completely shut down emotionally at an early age while growing up in this type of household. They essentially stop their emotional development and channel their energy into other life areas, which some feel happens through a process of "sublimation."[6] Sublimation is when unwanted emotions are redirected into something thought to be positive and worthwhile.

For example, earning money, working hard, gaining status or power, and achieving success may all be used as ways to avoiding feelings or conflicts. Emotions can be channeled into all sorts of activities. It's not necessarily bad to channel emotions into work—if it's not harming your relationships. And certainly all successful people don't have unresolved emotions. But our feelings can significantly influence and motivate our behaviors. Our goal should be to experience and manage them well so our present behavior is not controlled by past experiences.

Perhaps you are just coasting along in life, doing fine, when something big happens—a marriage or divorce, the birth of a child, a move to a new area, a new job, losing a loved one—and suddenly your emotional reactions can seem overwhelming. How will you manage? Will you work through the feelings to learn and grow, or will you channel the feelings into more achievement? Changing your childhood default mode may be necessary. Here's an example:

> Ken grew up in a chaotic, unpredictable household. His emotionally unstable mother alternated between being very loving and being mean, hurtful, and verbally abusive. Ken's father was an alcoholic. Although not violent, he was lost in his own world of self-pity and avoidance through drinking. As a result, Ken learned from an early age to fend for himself. By age eleven, he was managing his own life as best he could, and he wanted out—out of the house and out of the family. Ken focused on achievement in school and left for college on an academic scholarship at age seventeen.
>
> Ken was a straight-A student in college and went on to become a successful physician. Over his career, he channeled all of his emotions into his work, which resulted in his being the busiest and the most respected internist in town. All of his emotional stress and anxiety was sublimated into his office practice.
>
> At age fifty, Ken developed a severe form of rheumatoid arthritis that brought up strong feelings—intense anger, frustration, fear, and sadness—but also took away his ability to work long hours at the office. And working long hours had been his principal means of dealing with feelings. Forced to confront the now unavoidable feelings, he entered therapy on the verge of a nervous breakdown.

The problem with sublimation is that the individual doesn't grow and mature emotionally, and this can lead to a focus on objects rather than people. Some common behaviors linked to this lack of emotional maturity are the inability to tolerate conflict, always agreeing with others, inability to disagree without becoming angry, mistrusting the emotions

of themselves and others, avoiding intimacy, alienating others as a means
of protection, and needing to please others in order to be accepted. Some
people will suppress or deny negative emotions. The emotions don't go
away; instead, they're just bottled up. Gradually the emotional pressures
build until an emotional explosion occurs—perhaps in the form of
rage or a temper tantrum—often from a seemingly minor provocation.
Emotional explosions cause emotional damage to relationships just
as physical explosions cause physical damage. Sometimes these same
individuals also inadvertently suppress positive emotions and may be
unable to fully experience joy, happiness, and excitement. Therapy may
help to uncork the bottle, releasing and working through the emotions so
they don't continue to interfere with building strong relationships.

SELF-ASSESSMENT—EMOTIONAL ABUSE

When you were growing up:

- Did you learn that all emotions are bad and result in pain? Or
  perhaps that nothing good comes from expressing feelings?
- Were your emotions discounted/negated with the result that
  today you discount others' emotions?
- Were emotions viewed as a weakness; if so, do you maintain
  that opinion?
- Were emotions either never discussed or never expressed, leaving
  you afraid to identify, trust, and share your own emotions?

Reflect on your answers. Do you have a lot to learn about emotions
and need to work at fully experiencing, identifying, and expressing them?

CONDITIONAL LOVE

Conditional love is dependent on some other thing or condition. You can think of it as if the other party is saying, "I will love you if you do _____, and I will not love you if you do_____." Fill in the blanks yourself. Here are some common examples:

get good grades	fail a course
are quiet and neat	are boisterous and messy
do what I say	do your own thing

There is no doubt that unconditional love is best for kids, but you must be a very emotionally and spiritually healthy person to truly love anyone, even your children, unconditionally. No one's perfect, but some are better than others in this regard. We humans tend to assign some condition or performance standard, even if it's a small one, to love. If you are a person of faith, you may believe, as we do, that God is the only source of unconditional love.

Yet we can and should strive to be unconditional in our love. But environments of conditional love are common and are frequently at the root of some nonproductive behaviors. Growing up under parents who placed conditions on their love seems to be the most common underlying factor in Achievers seeking help.

Childhood is a time for learning. When the parents base love on performance, the children figure out very quickly, "To be loved I have to get good grades" or "make the varsity football team" or "be a cheerleader" or "homecoming queen," or whatever is important to the parent. The kids learn that only worldly achievement and productivity bring love from others.

When these same kids carry this learning into their adult life, they can become driven to achieve, accomplish, and succeed.[7] In this way, they feel that they earn the love of others. They may not even love themselves unless they deem themselves worthy through accomplishments.

This "I've got to earn love" mindset is frequently accompanied by fear—fear that the love will be taken away. Individuals may be constantly worried that their faithful, loving partner is going to leave them. This keeps them focused on achieving or performing to maintain the relationship and be accepted by others, always wondering: *Am I doing enough to maintain the love?* Of course, that's not what good relationships are about, and this performance focus winds up harming their relationships. Here's an example:

> For Casey's parents, straight As and high school valedictorian weren't good enough. Casey never heard "good job" or "we're proud of you" from her parents. Controlling and intrusive, they tended to dwell on her weaknesses, such as athletics, and to push her to improve any rare low marks in her coursework.
>
> At the university, she did well in class but wasn't used to the freedom. In the spring of her freshman year, she was briefly detained by the campus police after they were called to break up a drunken sorority party. Her parents went ballistic, threatening to withdraw their financial support over this mistake. In response, Casey ramped up her achievement drive, decided to stay at school over her summers, and graduated in just three years.
>
> Over the next five years, she was the epitome of accomplishment. Casey earned an MBA in night classes, was promoted to manager at her company, and even trained for and completed an Ironman triathlon. However, her love life was in the pits. Over this same time, she had three loser boyfriends—men who treated her poorly and accomplished very little themselves. These relationships were almost parasitic in nature.

When the third boyfriend abruptly left her after "borrowing" $5,000, Casey woke up and found a therapist who helped her learn to praise and accept herself, to be assertive and set healthy boundaries, and to be self-confident in relationships.

In this example, Casey had low self-esteem and was starved for real love. She attracted poor partners but stayed because she feared not having anyone. As she learned to love herself unconditionally and release the unconscious "love must be earned" training of her childhood, she became free to be more selective in dating.

This "love must be earned" mindset is quite common. In our story of Michael and Jessica, Michael thought Jessica would love him because of his career, money, and success. And indeed, those things did initially attract Jessica. Yet, in the long term, Michael's intense focus on his career harmed their marriage.

Jessica, on the other hand, learned during her childhood that the way to be appreciated is to take care of others. Here is what each of them grew up experiencing:

> As she learned to love herself unconditionally and release the unconscious "love must be earned" training of her childhood, she became free to be more selective in dating.

Michael was one of two boys in his family. His father was very intense and dominated the household. As a highly respected surgeon, he was always looking to climb the next rung on the ladder of professional prestige and to increase his power and income. Between first grade and Michael's high school commencement, the family moved four times in search of a better position for his dad. They settled in one place during Michael's junior year when his dad became chairman of surgery at an academic medical center.

At home, Michael's father was critical, controlling, and unemotional. He left for work early, came home late, and spent little time with his wife and two sons. The two brothers competed fiercely for their father's infrequent attention and praise. In fact, their father encouraged this competition. Michael, the older of the two, received little praise except for As on the report card, making the baseball team, and standing up for himself with teachers and kids. Although his father pressed him to confront others, he was punished if he stood up to his dad. To this day, Michael does not remember his father ever hugging him or saying, "I love you."

Michael's mother was supportive of, but subservient to, his father. She found fulfillment in her spouse's achievements and she was similarly sparse with encouragement and praise for the children. Michael's parents were well off but had few close friends and didn't invest much time with their extended family. He never saw his parents show affection, hug or kiss one another, or heard them talk about feelings. In his family, to show your emotions was to show your weakness.

Jessica didn't have the perfect childhood either. Her father was a salesman and on the road a lot. He was a much warmer person than Michael's father, but still somewhat cool and distant from his kids. Her mother was the stereotypical 1950s housewife, cooking, cleaning, and generally orienting her life toward the care of her husband—that is until her husband left the family and she was required to find employment and support her children. Jessica was called on to pick up the slack and to assume parental responsibilities while her mother was working. Her four younger brothers were rebellious and defiant of their mother, and Jessica often served as the peacemaker in her father's absence. With her husband gone, Jessica's mother turned to her for emotional support, and Jessica was praised for being the compliant "good girl." Her brothers had more privileges and less responsibility at home, because, as her mother explained it, "They're boys." Jessica wound up learning that the way to be loved was to take care of others' needs. On a positive note, growing up in a large family relying on one another, Jessica learned how to connect with others.

Childhood is the training ground for the adults we are to become. Michael and Jessica learned how to be the way they are. People like this must unlearn destructive patterns of relating, substituting more constructive behaviors in their place. This process is very difficult, can take a considerable amount of time and energy, and usually involves another person such as a pastor or counselor. The question for every "Michael" and "Jessica" is: *Am I willing to seek help?* If you can identify with either of them, what is your own answer to this question?

SELF-ASSESSMENT—CONDITIONAL LOVE

What did you learn about giving and receiving love from your childhood environment?

- Did you learn that love from others was contingent upon good performance and positive achievement?
- Did you learn that if you did what others wanted and expected of you then you would be loved?
- Did you learn that you only give love if you receive it in equal proportions?
- Did you perceive that love would only be given if you maintained a positive image and façade regardless of your true feelings?
- Did you learn not to trust or accept love because it could be taken away by any mistake or failure you might experience?

Conditional love is fairly common. We all need to learn to love others for who they are, not what they do. This applies to loving ourselves as well.

Enabling of Irresponsibility

Another theme common in Achievers experiencing a Power Failure is parental enabling of irresponsibility. Many high achievers had very little responsibility as children, or their responsibilities were oriented around their area of talent or achievement. For example:

> Sarah was a preteen tennis prodigy. Her parents raised her with no responsibility or accountability besides success on the tennis court. She had no household chores or other responsibilities. She was only expected to win matches, and she did. Gradually she became selfish and self-absorbed with a huge sense of entitlement to match. Sarah was often demanding, inconsiderate, and rude to others. Never did her parents call her on the carpet for this behavior, instead excusing it because "everyone knows that the top stars are temperamental."
>
> Sarah went on to play professional tennis where her game continued to improve, but her attitude didn't. She went through coaches and boyfriends seemingly as fast as tennis balls. Naturally, she lost a lot of opportunity to improve her game from good coaching, and she lost a lot of personal opportunity for love and happiness. And Sarah didn't really have any friends on or off the court.
>
> After eight years as a pro, her career peaked with only a few small tournament victories, and Sarah hit an emotional wall. Burned out on tennis, she quit the sport but had nowhere else to go and no inner reserves to tap. "No coach, no manager, no friends, and no hope" was how she put it when she made the call to a counselor.
>
> Over time, with the help of her counselor, Sarah realized that she had made tennis her entire life and grew emotionally to become less focused on tennis and less self-centered.

Gradually, she was able to work better with others and enjoy relationships, which led to a marketing position in the tennis equipment industry.

Parents like Sarah's may see their child's innate talent or ability as more important than everything else. In any event, the child grows up thinking that it's okay to misbehave, not follow rules, break the law, or be otherwise irresponsible. They think, "It's okay because I'm special!" The child doesn't mature emotionally, doesn't learn social skills, and avoids responsibility.

> When we choose to renew our mind with beneficial thoughts, the power to have a new and better life is astounding.

In some cases, it's not just the parents who create this problem for their children. Teachers, coaches, and even peers often play a role in turning prodigies into prima donnas. Many of their surrounding entourage may begin to accommodate their needs and make excuses for them, allowing them to focus on their unique ability. This may continue into adulthood for those at the very top.

As a result, these "special ones" don't learn to accept responsibility and grow up expecting others to accommodate their needs well into adulthood. In some cases, people develop a narcissistic personality and feel entitled to special treatment. You've encountered many examples of this behavior. Think about the talented free-agent athletes or the children of the super-rich with whom you're familiar. How many appear self-centered, entitled, and arrogant? Of course, it's easy to see others' shortcomings; the challenge is to be able to see the same qualities in yourself.

IT'S NOT ALL ABOUT YOUR PARENTS

Children have many influences in addition to their parents. Teachers, coaches, relatives, and others can make a major difference in a child's psychological development, for better or for worse. Many successful individuals credit a coach or teacher who encouraged them through their childhood difficulties. All too often, some adults may influence children in a negative way. But no matter what your childhood influences, you can learn to think and behave differently.

As a child, Daniel struggled with education. Growing up in a working class family, he somehow slipped through the cracks in the local school system and remained illiterate into the seventh grade, being "socially promoted" along the way. Classmates continually ribbed him for being "stupid," and class spelling bees were a particular source of shame and embarrassment. In speaking with his parents, his teachers confirmed that Daniel was never going to amount to much because of his poor intellect. Eventually Daniel was placed into special education classes, learned to read poorly, and graduated from high school.

By then Daniel had internalized the message, "I'm stupid and won't amount to much." He would never have applied to college but for the fact that he was subject to being drafted and sent to fight in the Vietnam War. Daniel figured college could be a way to avoid the draft for a year or so until he flunked out. It was quite a surprise when he was accepted (on probation) to a state university.

Upon admission, Daniel was scared, but he was also feeling a little liberated; after all, none of the other kids there knew how stupid he was. He decided to just fake it until he flunked out. The first semester he earned two Bs and two Ds. "I got lucky," he thought, but the second semester he again earned two Bs and two Ds, producing a passing GPA for his freshman year. Next year, the same thing happened; he had maintained a straight C average. Sitting alone one evening it occurred to him that he wasn't flunking out. "I am going to be a college graduate! I am not stupid!" he thought.

That thought—"I am not stupid"—literally transformed his life. He decided to apply himself and was earning all Bs with the occasional A by his junior year. After graduation and some work experience, Daniel returned to graduate school and then seminary, earning two master's degrees and a doctorate of ministry, and was ordained as a minister.

Although we have changed his name, Daniel's story is real and shows both the power of childhood influences and also the power that we have to break free of those influences to create a better future for ourselves. Daniel said, "Inside I still sometimes hear a little voice that says, 'You can't achieve much because you are stupid. What you have done is a fluke,' but I don't listen to it. I think old 'tapes' never fully go away. Those early tapes can form the foundation of who we believe we are, and we still have a tendency to live out those messages. But when we choose to renew our mind with beneficial thoughts, the power to have a new and better life is astounding."

CONCLUSION

Perhaps you grew up with chaos, conflict, and turmoil, only to become used to them and draw them into your relationships now. Consciously or subconsciously, people often seek situations that remind them of their past because they're familiar, even if they're unhealthy.

Or perhaps you are trying to rewrite your childhood history through your actions in today's relationships. Some adults are searching for a "better parent" for themselves in their relationships now. But adults need partners, not parents.

And individuals sometimes seek to avoid vulnerability and intimacy by finding someone who also has a hard time getting close. If you couldn't trust your parents and share emotions with them, chances are you'll avoid

Enabling Is Disabling

When we do too much for others too often, they stop doing things for themselves. They become dependent on our help and feel incapable of doing things on their own. We need to let others manage their own affairs, even if it means they fail sometimes. Competence and confidence come with our own efforts. Face your issues and let others face theirs.

sharing your emotions with others. Choosing a partner who is as emotionally insecure, or worse, allows both parties to avoid intimacy.

If you recognize your own childhood home life in any of these illustrations, don't let leftover hurt or anger with your parents keep you from healing. Raising children isn't easy. Essentially all parents are learning as they go along. Some are better than others.

A lot of people are carrying some emotional baggage from childhood into their relationships today. But the good news is that your childhood doesn't have to determine your future. Becoming aware of the issues, confronting them, and working through them enables individuals to live differently, choose different behaviors, and create a better future.

It is never too late to change. So, if you learned something harmful to relationship-building as a child, just acknowledge it, and learn something new and beneficial now. Lots of people have done it. You can, too.

THE BOTTOM LINE:

- Your childhood certainly influenced your personality, but it doesn't have to determine your future. You can understand the past, learn from it, and release it to change yourself and your future.
- You have the power to create a healthy family and leave a legacy of healthy relationships to your children.

Your history is not your destiny, *unless you choose* it to be.

Finding Fame, Losing Love

Money Can't Buy You Love

Maybe you're not just successful. Maybe you're wildly successful. You're at the top, and you've achieved power and wealth far beyond most ordinary people. Perhaps you're a Hollywood star or celebrity, a major leaguer, state governor, entrepreneur, or executive. You may have multimillions of dollars to your name. You've got a house on the West Coast, an apartment in New York City, a condo in Miami Beach, and a flat in London. You fly first class or by private jet, belong to three country clubs, dine in only the finest establishments, and party at the Super Bowl every year. You're living large!

Congratulations! Many people dream of success like that, and you've done it! *Now you must be extremely careful,* because you're also at your most vulnerable when it comes to relationships with your spouse and family. All of the personality factors described so far could be major issues for you; in fact, they may be what helped you to ascend to your pinnacle. You've probably worked hard, very hard to succeed. Do you have an insatiable hunger for achievement? Do you feel compelled to prove yourself through accomplishments, wealth, and fame? Are you an adrenaline junkie who is easily bored and only motivated by the next challenge? Despite your success, in quiet moments, when you're alone, do you still feel unfulfilled and dissatisfied with life? If so, you're likely to sacrifice your relationships on the altar of "more."

Yes, you have achieved great things and should find satisfaction in your accomplishments, but there is a fine line between justified pride and arrogance/self-centeredness. It starts with a feeling that "I deserve to be treated differently" or "Rules don't or shouldn't apply to me." After the harmful behavior starts, further thoughts come: "I'm not hurting anyone by my actions" and "No one else needs to know." But eventually they do know, and they are hurt.

> You have achieved great things and should find satisfaction in your accomplishments, but there is a fine line between justified pride and arrogance/self-centeredness.

This entitlement mindset is very common among super-rich or extremely powerful Achievers. In the process of making it big, which may have taken years of hard work or appeared to happen overnight, people can lose their perspective on life. Over time they may lose the morals, values, and integrity they once had that gave them a sense of fair play and provided some self-restraint, and they become self-centered, power-abusing tyrants at home and at work. Their Connector partners may be expected to behave more like servants than spouses. These relationships either don't last or become marriages of convenience.

Here's an example of a powerful young Achiever who loses his way:

> Jay was a national high school basketball superstar, and no one was surprised when he skipped college to go straight to the NBA—especially since he'd received a $1 million signing bonus and a five-year, multimillion-dollar deal. At nineteen, he was a millionaire, celebrity, and living in a big-city penthouse apartment.
>
> That was the high watermark for Jay. Always cocky as a high school star, his ego expanded rapidly under the initial

adoration of the hometown fans, but this only worsened his impulsivity and poor judgment. Over the next three years, his personal and professional life spiraled downward. His multiple bar fights, arrests, and allegations of sexual assault together with his poor on-court performance and blaming his teammates quickly soured the public enthusiasm for him.

The worst part is that many people were trying to help Jay. His parents, his coaches, and some of the players tried to reach him, but he just wouldn't listen. Eventually he was released early when his team invoked a morals clause in his contract. After languishing for a season, he was eventually picked up by another team for the league minimum salary with a requirement to seek therapy.

What is your situation? If you're at the top, you're most likely surrounded by people. Some are great people, perhaps your true friends and loved ones. Others are not so great; they're people who only want a piece of you. Call them what you want—groupies, gold diggers, parasites, wannabes, or hangers-on—to these folks you're just a ticket to ride. Unfortunately, even some of your family members might fall into this category. Like remoras stuck to a shark, they hang around you feeding off the scraps from your life instead of earning their own way.

> The money you provide doesn't create love. Time is still your most valuable asset. Spend it on relationships with your loved ones.

You will also have your own people and tons of them. A large personal staff is part of the deal. Life isn't simple when you have four houses and six imported cars. So you've got butlers, maids, drivers, gofers, and a manager or agency to manage your affairs. And of course you have retained the top lawyers, doctors, and other professionals needed to assist you in your complex life. People around you are doing for you and telling you what you want to hear.[1]

Here's the problem. Some of these people are going to present you with enormous temptations destructive to your relationships. Women will make passes at you. People will offer you opportunities for drugs, alcohol, sex, gambling, and other pleasures that you would never experience if you were an ordinary person. Perhaps this has already happened to you. You are facing major personal pressures that, if you yield to them, can destroy your marriage, family relationships, friendships, and your physical, emotional, and spiritual health.

This was true for Michael, our surgeon, and he wasn't even close to your level of status, wealth, and power. As the hospital hero, nurses admired him for his confidence and abilities, and many flirted openly with him. Meanwhile the hospital administrators, mindful of his contribution to their bottom line, catered to his sometimes unreasonable demands for equipment, staff, and perks. Michael basked in the attention and support, and this only exacerbated the frustration he felt from Jessica's lack of attention to him. You can see how easy it was for him to become entangled in an affair rather than to do the hard work on himself and his own marriage.

Others around you may be enablers who help you to engage in destructive behavior. In fact, people at the top often enlist their staff to aid in their own destruction. Do you have any fixers in your retinue, including: the lawyers that "take care of" the DUI, the agent that suppresses the drunken nightclub photos, and the personal assistant that pays off the women from affairs and one-night stands? Elvis's and Michael Jackson's physicians enabled their drug use. If you're not careful, your people will do that for you, too.

Realize that *none* of these people has *your* best interests at heart. Their relationship with you is all about meeting their own needs—perhaps material needs, such as money, or psychological needs, such as love or status. But often, you like these people. You want them around. Be careful that you don't create the team that drags you down. For example:

> Kevin was frustrated with his father's insistence that he learn the construction business from the ground up before moving into upper management. Kevin always had plans, big plans, as he would tell his wife Lisa. Suddenly, at age twenty-eight, Kevin got his chance when his parents were killed in a car accident and he inherited the family construction company.
>
> He dove in and never looked back. Becoming CEO, he was determined to grow this regional company into a national powerhouse and wouldn't take no for an answer. Over the next couple of years, he replaced his dad's old management team with younger, more aggressive executives personally loyal to him. By year five, the company had tripled in size and gone public, allowing Kevin to extract millions in cash while still retaining a controlling stake.
>
> At the office, Kevin was king. He provided himself every perk he could imagine with company funds—first-class travel, an imported car, frequent meals, fine clothes, and expensive haircuts. His team of executives consisted of well-paid yes-men and -women. None would risk their status and income by challenging Kevin's behavior. He was their meal ticket, and they were well fed.
>
> Kevin traveled a lot for business and he liked it. Often he was the center of attention. Of course, he stayed in five-star hotels and always enjoyed a fine meal and drinks at the end of the day, frequently with the companionship of younger women. Frequently on trips together, his executives knew about his affairs but helped him to cover his tracks. Eventually one of his vice presidents, a young, single man,

began to make sure that Kevin always had "the right kind of company" on every out-of-town trip.

Meanwhile, Lisa, who had accepted his travel and work schedule knowing that it came with the CEO territory, was noticing unpleasant changes in Kevin's behavior. Kevin had become more irritable, abrupt, and demanding at home, as well as secretive and defensive about his travel schedule or work hours. Kevin's marriage was crumbling and fell apart completely when the full story came out in the newspapers after his name and cell phone number were found in a high society madam's black book.

Stories like Kevin's are distressingly common. Hopefully you can avoid these temptations. Even so, you're used to giving orders, having it your way, and being waited on hand and foot. You're likely to be much more controlling than average. Don't lose yourself to this illusion of power

> Embrace humility to avoid self-destruction and to have healthy connections with people.

and greatness. Remember that your spouse, children, family, and friends are not your staff. Don't fall into the trap of thinking that you can hire and fire your family, or that family relationships are based on economics. The money you provide doesn't create love. Time is still your most valuable asset. Spend it on relationships with your loved ones.

When you're at the top, any emotional or spiritual weakness that you have will be sorely tested. We've all seen newspaper articles that follow the self-destructive and relationship-destroying behavior of some lottery winners or young millionaire athletes. So what's the answer? What are you going to do?

Your first step is to understand the danger, and acknowledge that you're not invincible. Weaknesses come with being human.

Understand that your best protection is to be as emotionally and spiritually healthy as possible. Just as a physically healthy person is better able to resist and recover from illness, an emotionally and spiritually healthy individual is better able to handle the stress of being at the top. Part of being emotionally and spiritually healthy is maintaining healthy relationships—relationships in which you are loved and encouraged, and in which you love and encourage others.

How do you become emotionally and spiritually healthy? Change the way you approach and experience life. Surround yourself with solid and healthy people. Nurture relationships with one or two wise and stable people with integrity and high moral standards, people who genuinely care about your well-being. Seek their advice. Talk with them about your life and how it's going. Consult them on important decisions. Let them hold you accountable. Let them tell you where you're going off track or might be in the wrong. While you may be used to making decisions alone, having the input of wise and trusted friends may save you.

> **Balance Leads to Lasting Success**
>
> You can get pretty far in life on a few strong traits—ambition, drive, and intelligence, to name several. But what about your weaknesses? They can destroy your success in a flash. You may be unbalanced by your lack of emotional maturity, and when you're off balance, you're ready to fall. It's better to be balanced. A life of significance comes from positively affecting others. Significance requires balance. Be balanced.

Be careful about the places you go, the things you do, and the people you hang out with. If you're honest with yourself, you know the situations where you are especially vulnerable and likely to get in trouble—avoid them like the plague! Of course, alcohol and drugs can be problems for everyone. You're no different.

Living more cautiously and maintaining accountable relationships can be hard for anyone, and the critical element is your attitude. If you believe that "I'm better or smarter than other people" or "My time is more valuable than anyone else's time," you won't be able to manage, and you will create problems in all of your relationships. Embrace humility to avoid self-destruction and to have healthy connections with people. Be more grateful for than proud of your achievements, and acknowledge all the people who helped make it happen for you. Don't forget where you came from and who you were before you hit it big.

Get your focus off yourself for a while. Take a look around and involve yourself in the lives of others in a positive way. Divert some of your vast resources to giving back through time, talent, or money. Any new activity where you can just be an ordinary person will help you stay grounded and develop an identity separate from your success. A moderate diversity of activities will create a more sustainable, stable, and balanced life. Stay on your feet and grounded despite your success. Without balance, you're set up for a fall.

And don't forget to nurture your faith and connection to a power greater than yourself. Joining a house of worship, regularly attending services, participating in a small group study and individual spiritual study, and prayer are ways to deepen your relationship with God. There is nothing more important.

If you don't think of yourself as a person of faith, then grapple with the big issues in life. Your time on earth is short. Why are you here? What does your life mean? What is important and what is not important in your life? Too many people at the top never even ask these questions, yet answering them is the beginning of wisdom. We all have to figure out our own answers, but taking the questions seriously may be the best thing you ever do to stay at the top in life.

THE BOTTOM LINE:

- Wealth, power, and fame make people more vulnerable to relationship-destroying behaviors—the more wealth, power, and fame, the more vulnerable.
- Pride goes before a fall. Work to stay humble. Be thankful for your success, and give back to others. Don't let it all go to your head. Never forget where you came from.
- Grow spiritually. Find meaning in life. Understand that you are important for being human and for who you are— not for your money, power, and fame.

Balance
breeds success.

Falling In Love Again

Steps to Achieving Connection

There is no single "ideal marriage." Your ideal marriage is simply the relationship that works best for you and your spouse. It will most likely have these characteristics.

You and your spouse like each other, spend time together, and enjoy each other's company. You are emotionally intimate, sharing your hopes, fears, and dreams in a way that you don't with anyone else. Physical intimacy is present, too—hugs, kisses, holding hands, backrubs, and sex. And the sex is enjoyable, for both of you.

The two of you know that conflicts or disagreements are part of life and a normal part of marriage, too. As a result, you're able to talk things through and work out a practical solution, even if is to agree to disagree.

Sometimes feelings are bruised, but you each are able to accept responsibility, apologize, and let go—choosing forgiveness over nursing grudges. There is no blaming, and neither of you ever lashes out at the other, shuts down, pouts, or sulks. You trust each other.

Each of you is a complete, whole person who is not needy or dependent. Nevertheless, you both recognize that your relationship is more important than outside issues that arise in life—work, friends, family, and hobbies. You both *want* to be married as opposed to *need* to be married. You choose to share your life with the other.

Because you recognize that you are two separate individuals choosing to be a couple, you don't expect your partner to complete you or enjoy all of your interests. So, despite your closeness, you are still two separate people with individual tastes, hobbies, and friends.

Neither of you tries to control the other. Rather, you support each other's separateness and give each other space in which to enjoy life apart from the marriage relationship. You each experience joy in life with your partner, with your friends, and when you're alone.

Think of it like ballroom dancing. To be fluid and graceful, the partners must be in step with one another the whole time. Each is moving differently from the other, but each partner's movements are in concert with and in support of the other's. As a result, they can dance beautifully as a couple.

Maybe you went through a rough spell or two during your courtship or earlier in your marriage, but now your relationship is working. And it seems to be getting better every year. You hope that your children will have the kind of relationship with their spouses that you have with yours.

In summary, you like your spouse, you love your spouse, and you're in love with your spouse—"like" meaning you enjoy his or her company, "love" meaning you have a strong feeling of caring for him or her, and "in love" meaning you have a deep affection for him or her as well.

BACK TO REALITY

However, marriage is not something that comes naturally to most people. Few couples like, love, and remain deeply in love with each other throughout every moment of their relationship. Often the feelings come and go over time. It seems that it's easy to fall out of love or even to stop liking your partner while still loving them as a person.

So the question for most couples is, "Can we get those feelings back?" Absolutely! Partners can rekindle the strong feelings they've had for each other in the past. The real issues are how long the feelings have been draining out of the relationship and how committed the partners are to making it work. When couples put time, effort, and energy into their marriage, they can fall in love all over again.

Cultivating any relationship is similar to cultivating a garden. Gardens need regular weeding, watering, fertilizing, and pruning to be at their best. Similarly, all relationships require regular time and attention to flourish. And your marriage should be the best relationship you have.

So it follows that your marriage might require the most work. That's true. A relationship needs time, effort, and energy from both partners to thrive. The good relationships you may admire in others are almost always the result of hard work. All long-married couples have faced relationship challenges, which they had to work out, sometimes with the help of a marriage counselor. Your relationship with your spouse will likely be the most challenging personal relationship you'll ever have, but it should also be the most fulfilling. And it can be, if you do the work. As with any relationship, marriage flourishes with attention, respect, trust, and love.

Think of it like ballroom dancing. To be fluid and graceful, the partners must be in step with one another the whole time. Each is moving differently from the other, but each partner's movements are in concert with and in support of the other's. As a result, they can dance beautifully as a couple.

Marriage is similar. For a successful marital dance, both spouses must act in concert with and in support of the other. They express their own individuality, but always in the context of the larger marital bond. During hard times such as illness, loss, or emotional problems, one person may help pull the other along but can't completely take over for their partner. If either one ever chooses to just "do my own thing," a crash is in the offing.

Every marriage has its ups and downs. Even in strong marriages, partners find that passion, excitement, and connectedness change over time. Don't misinterpret this as a huge problem. Some detect less passion or excitement and, without realizing how typical it is, decide their marriage is on the rocks and begin to detach—thereby creating a self-fulfilling prophecy. Don't detach; just give it some time and take steps to reestablish closeness.

It simply isn't realistic to expect to feel the same intensity of love and attraction every day that you felt on your wedding day. In any relationship, at times one person may love his or her partner more than his or her partner loves back. Over time, this love discrepancy alternates back and forth between the partners. If this is you, that's okay. Similar to ballroom dancing, as long as the distance between you doesn't become too great and you're still moving in support of each other, you're probably doing fine.

Sometimes people do fall out of love with each other. If this seems to be happening, don't panic. The important question is, what do you do about the loss of connection? How long do you let it go before taking action? Some individuals turn outward, seeking other people or things to fill the void. In a healthy marriage, the partners turn inward and make positive changes, which brings the feelings back. When partners need help, counseling can assist them in reestablishing a deep connection of love, but it must start with their commitment to the relationship and to each other.

In our initial story, Michael and Jessica had fallen out of love at least several years before their crisis. Perhaps it started upon Michael's beginning private practice and spending longer hours at the hospital. Or maybe it began as Jessica's focus shifted to work at the wellness center and the children's activities. Or, perhaps more likely, both were factors. Regardless, Michael and Jessica became caught up in the busyness of their lives and didn't realize until later that their love for each other had faded.

For years, their marriage was receiving very little energy from either of them. It just got the little bit left at the end of the day. In the end, they drifted apart, and each filled the void with other things or other people.

Now What?

So your marriage isn't perfect. And you're asking, "What should I do? How do I work on my relationship?" The answer is to take responsibility for only yourself and work on the five essentials that were covered earlier:

1. Partnership of Equals
2. Marriage Is a Priority
3. Effective Communication and Conflict Resolution
4. Forgiveness and Trust Building
5. Intimacy

It's best if you and your partner can agree to do this together, but often, that's not what happens. People wait too long to address any issues in their relationship and become too disconnected to begin working together. If this is you, you may find it helpful to seek marriage counseling or therapy. Go by yourself and get individual therapy if you must. Just start.

Avoiding Pain Causes Pain
Disagreement can be acutely painful. But unresolved conflict builds resentment and chronic pain. With each new unresolved issue, this chronic pain accumulates, and relationships suffer. Resolving disagreements is essential to all healthy relationships. We grow through this process and model helpful behaviors for our children. Work through your conflicts.

Of course, avoiding the pain of a problematic relationship can be easier than confronting it and working through the issues. Unfortunately, failing to address the core issues often leads to recurring problems in relationships. For example:

Shane had been described as cool and distant his whole life. Nevertheless, as a handsome and successful attorney, attracting girlfriends was not a problem. Keeping them was another issue, and he went through at least one a year. Usually they broke up with him because of his coolness and insensitivity, but he wasn't one to get depressed or even sad. He just found a new woman.

Eventually a combination of wanting a real family and meeting Beth, his "perfect match," led him to the altar at age forty-two. By his forty-fifth birthday, it was all over. Beth filed for a no-fault divorce and it went quickly. Shane followed his prior pattern and moved on. Within two years, he married Angela, a successful businesswoman who was twice divorced herself. Predictably, their marriage also hit the rocks relatively quickly, but at age fifty-three, Shane decided that he wanted to be married and finally sought help for himself and his marriage.

Stories like Shane's are rather common among successful lawyers, doctors, and businesspeople. They've failed in multiple relationships and have never figured out what went wrong. They rarely ask, "What was my role in the situation? How can I be better?" Instead, they just move on, often blaming the other party and looking for the "right person" for their next relationship. It doesn't work like that. So whatever effort and help it takes for you to be healthy as an individual and couple, make that investment before it is too late.

HOW THERAPY WORKS

Many couples or individuals who could benefit from therapy don't seek help for many reasons. One is pride. It can hurt to admit that you need help from someone else or that your marriage isn't perfect. This may be especially true for Achievers who are used to being in control and solving their own problems. They are typically reluctant to be vulnerable and may see these admissions as signs of weakness.

Sometimes individuals can admit their problems to themselves, but they remain too concerned about appearances. They may feel a stigma associated with counseling. "Who will find out about this?" "What if I see someone I know in the waiting area?" These are the kind of thoughts that perpetuate the problem.

Money is an issue for some potential clients. Counseling does cost money, and they can't afford it or believe they can't. This is a real problem for many but would not be typical of the Achievers we're describing. Add to that the fear of the unknown. In reality, most people don't know what to expect from marriage counseling.

Seeing a counselor means admitting you're not perfect and that you need help with your relationship. Some perceive this as a weakness and can't imagine sharing intimate information with a complete stranger, but making the decision to pursue counseling is a sign of strength and maturity. Individuals in need of help who don't seek counseling often continue to repeat the same unproductive behavior and create more turmoil in their lives.

> Making the decision to pursue counseling is a sign of strength and maturity.

High achievers can have an especially difficult time acknowledging problems and accepting that they need an outsider's help. After all, they solve complicated problems every day, so why is this any different?

Others talk themselves out of therapy with thoughts like, "I won't learn anything I don't already know." Or "It will be useless. My spouse is the problem and won't change." Or "I can't change. Why try?" Erase these thoughts from your mind. They're not helpful, and they're not accurate, either. You really don't know what might happen in therapy or what you might be willing and able to change about yourself. People can change.[1] That includes you!

Counseling is much more than just talking, and it's not about blaming yourself or anyone else. It's about learning new skills, understanding yourself, and changing for the better. *Consumer Reports* has endorsed the efficacy of therapy based on a survey of four thousand readers who sought mental health services. They found that therapy for emotional problems can have a substantial beneficial effect.[2] Others have also confirmed that psychotherapy works.[3,4] No one can change the past, but counseling can help you change your life from today forward.

Of course, therapy is professional and confidential. The therapist is not supposed to be your friend. He or she has a single purpose—to help you to achieve your goals. An effective counselor should be honest and direct with you, have your best interests at heart, and maintain complete confidentiality.

While each therapist has his or her own approach, effective therapy will help people understand their need for deep and long-lasting change, and that if they are motivated and treat counseling as a serious matter, they can make tremendous strides to transform their relationships and their lives. One common and effective counseling approach is called cognitive behavioral therapy, which may be blended with other techniques as therapy progresses. This method involves two broad steps: raising awareness of thought and behavior patterns, and then changing those patterns. Insight into the problems is helpful, but good strategies and actions are required to create and reinforce new thoughts and behavior. Here's how it works:

SETTING THE STAGE

Counseling usually begins with a phone call asking for help, most often from the most relationship-oriented partner, which in the A/C marriage is usually the Connector. Sometimes couples come together, but most often the individuals meet with the therapist separately at first, with the understanding that their long-term success with this process will ultimately involve joint therapy. The goal at this first visit is to understand the "whole person" who represents half of the marriage. There may be a lot to understand—medical issues, psychiatric issues, childhood experiences, habits, life experiences, prior relationships, personality traits, and goals for therapy all are a part of this assessment.

Many questions need to be answered: How much conflict was each individual exposed to as a child? How was conflict resolved or not in the home? What was the level of emotional intimacy, affection, and connection among the parents and children while growing up? What is the degree of commitment to the marriage, and are there any present-day destructive behavior patterns? By the end of this hour, a skilled counselor will have identified many themes in the individual's

Blame Prevents Change
Ultimately, your life is about what you choose to do. You can't control others' actions or inactions. Blaming others takes your focus off your own choices and abilities. So you can get stuck waiting for others to change, because "it's their fault." Drop the blame, focus on what you can do, and make it happen.

dating or marriage history, and their basic personality traits. If the first counseling session(s) involve only one individual, a counselor often will encourage him or her to share with their partner what has been gained.

The first joint session often sets the tone for the course of therapy. A counselor must remain neutral, objective, and nonjudgmental in delivering his or her impressions and recommendations. At this point, the counselor will discuss what he or she feels has contributed to the marriage going awry and propose a plan of therapy. This meeting can be emotionally charged and very tense. The individuals may have trouble even being in the same room together and may even sit in opposite corners. Other symptoms of the level of tension are often revealed by the clients' body language and other nonverbal clues as the counselor seeks to create a safe environment of support where the parties can really understand and even discuss their own roles in the situation.

Sometimes the issue is major relationship-destroying behavior on the part of one or both parties—things like infidelity, verbal and emotional abuse, physical abuse, alcoholism, drug addiction, or other addictive behavior. Your marriage cannot be strong when these issues are present. But in most cases, the problem is less formidable. For example, the couple has neglected their marriage in favor of work, status, possessions, and children as substitutes for working on emotional and physical intimacy. As with Michael and Jessica, the marriage was placed on autopilot, and the couple drifted apart over months and years until the eventual detachment behaviors caused a crisis.

Whatever the issues, the goal is to identify them all—not for blaming, but for understanding. Marriage is a two-person relationship, and therapy requires the commitment of both individuals. They must be committed to work on the relationship and to change only themselves. Often there already have been years of blaming and keeping score in the relationship, and more of that isn't going to help.

Sometimes one party is really not invested in changing and has already checked out of the marriage. He or she is only here to reduce their guilt and "check the box" before divorce court. They're thinking, "I want to be able to say that I gave therapy a chance and it didn't work. Now I can get a divorce." Should the therapist discern this, a limited trial of therapy may be suggested, to help determine the likelihood of the parties successfully working through their issues. Or one party may have so much anger, resentment, or hurt that individual therapy is needed first for any hope of beneficial couples work later. And some individuals have independent psychological issues and problems that justify individual therapy, either by a separate therapist or in conjunction with the couple's work together.

Once everything is on the table, the therapist will propose a plan of action for improvement, reminding the couple that therapy is an action-based process that is primarily forward looking. It's about what to do to get better, doing it, and getting better. The plan for therapy is specific with major goals, intermediate objectives, and clear directions that can help the couple get through this difficult time. If individual work with one partner is needed, it is usually centered around self-knowledge and self-control. For the couple's work to proceed, each individual must have at least a moderate ability to understand and manage their own thought patterns and behavior in a way that supports joint therapy. This may require a little dialing up or down of certain personality traits, resolving issues or conflicts from the past, and gaining interpersonal skills.

GETTING STARTED

Now the work starts. While *the therapist provides insight, strategy, direction, and guidance in the therapeutic process, ultimately it's* the responsibility of each individual to work on himself or herself and to work on the relationship together. This is frequently *very painful,* but healing usually accompanies the suffering. Facing the pain is critical, because it was the avoidance of the anticipated pain of working through issues that created the crisis in the first place.

Improving communication skills *(especially listening)* lays the foundation for progress. It's rather common for couples to think they communicate adequately when, in fact, neither actually truly listens when the other speaks. Good listening requires them not to interrupt each other and to remain attentive to the entire conversation. It's also common for what conversation there is to be very superficial or logistical in nature, and this simply doesn't help to forge emotional

> **Speak It to Solve It**
>
> Conflicts occur between people, and people need to talk things out. Many individuals are reluctant to talk with their partners about the issues important to them. Think before you speak, but speak. Get the conflict out of your head and into your mouth. Talk about your disagreements.

bonds. Deeper and more intimate conversations are needed to foster feelings of love and connection.

The following exercises and actions have been found to help:

> As a couple, set aside twenty minutes three times each week to sit down for a conversation with no distractions. Get a pillow from the couch to designate who has the floor. Speak only when you have the pillow, and after two or three minutes of speaking, stop and pass the pillow to your partner. The listening partner should then ensure understanding through paraphrasing and clarifying questions such as, "So I'm hearing that you're feeling _____ because _____. Is that right?" Validation statements, such as, "I understand how you might feel that way," are also very helpful. Take turns expressing a concern or issue and ensuring that you understand and validate your partner's thoughts and feelings.

> Call a time-out if you get in a heated or prolonged argument. Either party may call the time-out, and the other should respect that. Go to separate areas of the house for fifteen to sixty minutes to allow yourself to cool down.

> The point of the time-out is to avoid a blow up, not to avoid a resolution, and you will need to come back to the discussion. So take the opportunity to cool down, gather your thoughts and composure, and perhaps even write down your thoughts and feelings. Then the person who called the time-out should reconvene the conversation.

> Take responsibility for your own feelings. When speaking about your feelings, use "I" statements rather than blaming your feelings on your partner. For example, "I feel ignored and angry when you come home late without calling" rather than "You are ignoring me and making me angry when you come home late without calling."

And try to avoid the absolute words like "always" and "never." They're never accurate. Nobody "always" does anything. These words can provoke intense emotional reactions. You are trying to communicate, not fight.

Depending on the exact situation, the relationship toolbox will include many more exercises, tips, and techniques for the couple to use in improving communication. This stage usually lasts about a month, and it's not always smooth sailing. Very often, the first two or three couples sessions are quite combative. The pent-up anger and frustration of both spouses finally explodes outward. With the shouting, blaming, accusing, and vicious put-downs, it's sometimes an hour of pure pain. Perhaps this is how the individuals have been interacting for many months, which gives the therapist a glimpse of their at-home behavior. But only after the feelings are out and productively addressed can the healing begin.

Resentment-Anger with a History

We all get angry with others from time to time. But what do you do with anger once you have it? There are two main options. You can work through the anger, express it constructively, and release it. You're then free to be happy and enjoy the relationship again. Or you can hold on to it, nurse a grudge, and build resentment. Resentment kills relationships. Say what you need to say constructively, and then let it go.

Debbie and Brad were in their fourth visit when Debbie's long-simmering anger boiled over. As she ratcheted up the intensity, finally screaming at Brad, the therapist leaned over to her and whispered, *"I can't hear you,"* which stopped her cold. *"What?"* she replied. *"Debbie, when you shout like that my natural inclination is to cover my ears. Chances are that Brad is tuning you out as well."* Debbie got the point.

Often, how we say things is more important than what we say. Our style and nonverbal messages may have a dramatic impact, for better or worse, on those with whom we're speaking. Learning a new style, lowering the tone, and choosing better words can lead to huge improvements in our interactions.

One of the nice things about marital therapy is that the results are usually obvious to everybody. As the couple puts energy into these exercises, the therapist can see and hear the difference in the sessions. He or she sees the body language reflect less anger and hostility. Follow-up comments are heard, like: "It's nice not to be fighting" and "We're talking a lot more. We haven't talked like this in years!" or "I'm really enjoying being with him/her now." And he finds the individuals less self-absorbed, perhaps one of them noticing artwork or plants in the office for the first time. Things are going well when this is happening.

BUILDING ON THE FOUNDATION

After communication comes constructive conflict resolution, a major issue for couples experiencing the Power Failure Syndrome. Their lack of exposure to successful conflict resolution has often left them conflict-averse and afraid of this phase of therapy.

Up to the point of a relationship crisis, many high achievers have learned to approach arguments with the goal of winning, not compromising. They may be more concerned about making their point and getting the other person to agree than understanding another perspective. Many couples in therapy have spent way too long arguing about who's right rather than trying to accept their differences and agree on a common plan of action.

We all have our own perceptions, ideas, and biases, and we all want to be listened to and heard when expressing our opinions. The following seven-step method will help each party hear the other person and acknowledge their viewpoint before negotiating a solution. Most couples find it feels safe and even comfortable, unlike their prior history with attempts at conflict resolution.

SEVEN STEPS TO SUCCESSFUL CONFLICT RESOLUTION

1. Identify the conflict in concrete terms. Avoid vague generalities. Specify exactly what behaviors are at issue. How are they measured? You must agree on the conflict before moving to the next step.
2. Identify and express your emotions related to the conflict.
3. Validate your partner's emotions by acknowledging and accepting their feelings even if you don't agree.
4. Brainstorm possible solutions to the conflict and write down the various options.
5. Negotiate the various choices by presenting the pros and cons for each.
6. Work toward a compromise, being flexible and open to selecting an option that meets the needs of both parties.
7. Implement the selected solution, release any negative emotion, and let go of the conflict. Agree to the mutual goal of achieving closure and not revisiting the issue.[5]

The first and last steps of the seven-step conflict resolution strategy are often the most difficult. Couples typically don't recognize the deeper issues fueling their arguments and have a difficult time letting go of past hurts. In some cases, there is more than one conflict, which requires the couple to go through the steps twice. The closure comes not from the choice you've selected, but from the process of discussing all emotions and options openly.

> Marie and Bob fought daily over how to raise the kids. Superficially, the conflicts were about TV time, chores, manners, and the like, but the deeper issues were Marie's domineering style and Bob's passive-aggressive response.

Working through the conflict using the seven steps allowed these issues to surface.

Marie felt that she had to do all the work of raising their three children because of Bob's lack of effort. Meanwhile, Bob felt frustrated that Marie always critically rejected his parenting, and in response, he had shut down in that area years ago. Each had grown very resentful of the other. Once this was out in the open, they could focus more on changing themselves to solve the deeper issues, which allowed them to resolve parenting differences quickly and without rancor.

FORGIVENESS—LETTING GO OF THE PAST

Forgiveness is the most difficult and painful, yet *most essential*, step in therapy. As the couple works toward mutual forgiveness, they each must revisit the pain, hurt, anger, sadness, guilt, fear, and resentment they've experienced over their years of marital dysfunction.[6] Since it is important to accomplish this in a controlled manner, it is usually done in-session.

> No one can obtain the trust of their spouse by demanding it; they can only act in a trustworthy manner and allow it to develop.

Over the life of a marriage, there can be many things that need to be forgiven. Outright verbal and emotional abuse, emotional withdrawal, physical withdrawal through overinvolvement in work or hobbies, excessive spending, lack of effort to maintain the home or marriage, withholding of sex, alcoholism or drug addiction, pornography, and infidelity are common issues in troubled relationships. Not all marital mistakes or transgressions are the same—there are mistakes, and then there are MISTAKES. By anyone's standards, adultery is a MISTAKE. Can couples successfully overcome the devastation of an extramarital affair, or other major issue, to have a lasting and vibrant marriage? Yes, couples can heal from adultery and other MISTAKES, but it takes hard work. Both parties must want the relationship to succeed, take responsibility for their own actions, work to change themselves, and be willing to forgive their partner. To prepare for a session that deals with one or more MISTAKES, a therapist might ask a couple:

Before our next session, please write two letters. Address the first letter to your spouse and describe the experiences and events of your relationship and the actions of your partner that have led to your feelings today. Do not shy away from the tremendous hurt, pain, anger, sadness, or resentment that you have or have had along the way. It's vital that each of you describe your feelings openly, directly, and completely. Then tell your spouse that you are choosing to let go of the pain of the past and that you are forgiving them.

By forgiving, you mean you are releasing the emotional pain, letting it go, and deciding to move forward without continuing to revisit it. You might think of it as giving up the desire to get even.

Additionally, you're not promising to ignore behavior that is still going on. You need only forgive what has happened in the past, keeping in mind that forgiveness and trust are not identical. You may not trust your partner right now. That will come later. While you will probably always remember these events, you can be released of their emotional hold on you.

Address the second letter to yourself. Write about your own mistakes, poor decisions, and inappropriate behavior, and the emotional pain they have created for you and your family. Then, just as you expressed forgiveness to your spouse, forgive yourself. Let go of your guilt, shame, anger, or frustration with yourself. Self-forgiveness is necessary for your own emotional growth, upon which the growth of the relationship depends.

At our next session, you will each read your letters aloud to your spouse and yourself, and we will spend some time understanding and working through your feelings.

Some couples balk at this exercise and they need some time to process the very idea of it before they can actually take this step. The actions of writing these two letters, reading them with your partner in-session, and discussing them is indeed *very* powerful.

> **Holding On to the Past Keeps It in the Present**
> Why do we tell ourselves that we can't get over the past? There are so many examples of people who have done so. Are we so different from them? Being stuck in the past prevents us from enjoying the present. Getting over your past is a choice. Make it and grow. Let the past be past.

Everyone needs to be aware that forgiveness doesn't usually happen all at once, but that the letters are a way to get the healing process moving forward. Identifying the depth of the pain is very important. Since it hurts so much, the individuals may never have been able to fully confront their emotional pain, especially in a calm and direct manner. And many people don't know what they're feeling, only that it hurts. By reflecting and naming their emotions, they can more easily let them go.

Some are not ready to actually forgive their spouse because they're worried that he or she might do it again, and they don't want to let their guard down. Of course, if their partner isn't sorry and hasn't changed, it's understandable why they might not be ready to forgive. That's okay. The letter-writing exercise can be a way of increasing their readiness to forgive later.

This method is useful with individuals, even if their spouse does not participate. Writing, reading, and role-playing with letters can help release enormous amounts of pain that had been preventing emotional growth. Here's a fictional example of a letter from Sam to Laura:

Dear Laura,

There are some things I've been holding on to over the years of our marriage and I need to say them so I can let them go. I've always loved you, but I can't trust you anymore and I'm not sure we can make it together as a couple. My therapist told me to write this letter to release my negative feelings. Going forward, even if we divorce, I want to be at peace myself, and to be able to be civil with you for the sake of our children.

Frankly, our children deserve better than the relationship we've had. I want them to grow up happy and healthy, and to have good marriages. They are old enough to pick up on our feelings for each other and we can't pretend that our marriage is happy and healthy. I'm tired of arguing with you in front of the kids and I know it's hurting them.

What hurts me the most is your affair. I never thought you would do such a thing. I'm not perfect, but how could you do this to me? What was missing from our marriage that you thought you could find elsewhere? I know I work a lot and I'm not a talker like you are, but that doesn't make it right to have an affair.

Finding those e-mails and text messages to Bob was devastating. I was in shock when his wife called and confirmed everything in detail, and she told me that everyone knew but me. I am still embarrassed, humiliated, angry, and hurt. I still can't believe that you would stoop that low. I thought you had more class and better morals than that. How can I ever trust you again? You keep saying that it's over, but how can I trust you? You lied to me for six months, maybe more. Maybe you still are lying now.

I appreciate that you broke it off with Bob with me on the line and have given me full access to your e-mail and cell phone. It also helps that you have taken responsibility for your actions and seem to be sorry. What helps the most is that you will go for individual therapy, too. I hope you figure out why you did what you did.

I forgive you for the affair. I know we have been under a lot of stress with the children and our jobs. I want to work through this and everything and try to save our marriage. I'm hopeful that we can do it, but it depends on you, too.

I will work on trusting you, but it's going to take me some time. I will stop throwing the affair in your face to make you feel guilty. I also know that I have some changing to do. I love you and want to make this work.

Love, Sam

Rebuilding trust is another matter. No one can obtain the trust of their spouse by demanding it; they can only act in a trustworthy manner and allow it to develop. When individuals can't trust their partner to be there for them, to support them, and to support the relationship, they can't let their emotional guard down. They might express it like this, "How can I share my feelings with him? He'll just laugh them off and, worse, tell his buddies like he's done before." Without trust, it is next to impossible to have a healthy marriage.

Lack of trust harms relationships in two very different ways. The usual way is through the "emotional poisoning" of constant suspicion. Almost everyone resents not being trusted, even if they aren't actually trustworthy! Gradually,

> **Forgiveness Is a Choice**
> "I just can't forgive him (or her)." Of course it's not true. You can choose to forgive anyone for anything. Or you can choose to hold on to your anger, hurt, and resentment. Forgiveness doesn't excuse bad behavior. It doesn't mean that there may not be consequences for the forgiven action, but it allows the forgiver to heal and move on with his or her life. Forgiving empowers the forgiver, enabling him/her to release the pain. Empower yourself through forgiveness.

the resentment will build as they chafe under what seems like constant surveillance or the feeling that they have to measure up somehow.

The other potential outcome is less common, with one partner who overcompensates with enabling behavior to avoid the need for trusting the other. Essentially he or she is drawn into controlling behaviors in an attempt to ensure outcomes for which they can't trust their partner. Here's an example:

> Cathy loved her alcoholic husband, Tim, very much, but he just couldn't stop drinking on his own. He'd be sober for a week or two and then go right back to the bars for a month. Gradually, Cathy began to orient her behavior around keeping Tim away from whiskey. Clearly, she couldn't trust him to do it himself.
>
> Cathy monitored Tim closely, checking on him at least several times a day, by phone and occasionally in person. She drove him to the factory where he worked, and picked him up at closing time. If he wasn't out the door promptly, she'd begin to get anxious, assuming the worst.
>
> Eventually this obsession affected her relationships and her physical health. She lost a lot of her friends, stopped her workouts, and gained fifteen pounds. She couldn't sleep either, for fear that Tim would get up in the middle of the night to drink secretly.

You can see how Cathy's enabling behavior prevented her and Tim from developing a healthy relationship. For this to happen, Cathy needed to trust Tim. Whether or not Tim would remain sober was Tim's issue. This sounds harsh, but for a chance to heal, partners must begin to trust one another again. If it turns out that the trust is not justified, the relationship may indeed dissolve, but this is a risk that many individuals, like Cathy, must take in order to give the relationship a chance to survive.

Often partners choose to trust a little bit at a time and then see what happens. They may be quite anxious doing this at first, but over time if the trust is not violated, they usually relax and trust more.

With persistence, trust can be rebuilt. Here are some suggestions about how to do that:

TRUST-BUILDING BEHAVIORS

- Be honest, open, and direct
- Mean it when you say yes
- Be able to say no
- Accept no when you hear it from your partner
- Initiate connection through activities and words
- Be vulnerable and disclose your thoughts, fears, and feelings
- Acknowledge and accept your shortcomings
- Be sorry and say it, if appropriate
- Avoid defensiveness and justification
- Don't resort to blaming
- Release emotional pain
- Confront and resolve conflict
- Forgive yourself and others
- Be consistent in your words and deeds
- Accept responsibility for your actions, positive and negative

REBUILDING INTIMACY

Only after a great deal of forgiveness and the appearance of a little trust are most couples ready to work on rebuilding intimacy. Intimacy is feeling a close connection with another person based on acceptance, understanding, transparency, dialogue, and reciprocity. In an intimate relationship, you can be yourself, share your thoughts and feelings, and be vulnerable with acceptance and love. Intimate partners stay connected even during difficult times, and they are forgiving. Couples in an intimate relationship accept their partner's individuality and integrate those differences into the relationship.

Often the first goal in recreating intimacy in a relationship is just to get both parties to understand they may be approaching this differently. Connectors may prefer to connect emotionally before becoming physically intimate while Achievers may go about it in the opposite direction. The best outcome is achieved through mutual understanding and flexibility on the part of both individuals. Each may never fully understand their partner but can learn to appreciate and respect their differences.

> Intimacy is feeling a close connection with another person based on acceptance, understanding, transparency, dialogue, and reciprocity.

Expressing your feelings openly and directly creates greater connection and closeness in a relationship. You can be vulnerable and be yourself. You can develop strategies together to become more physically connected. It's good if these ideas are fun and lead to excitement and passion. Here are some examples real couples have used:

- Take a walk on the beach (or in the woods)
- Go for a bike ride
- Attend a concert, movie, or play
- Have a cup of coffee together
- Garden together in the yard
- Go out to lunch or breakfast
- Shop together at the mall
- Make a day trip to a theme park

It's not that hard for people to come up with shared activities that they really will enjoy. After all, that's often how they fell in love in the first place.

That's therapy in a nutshell. It ends when the couple is progressing well on their own. The time this takes, from initial visit to termination of counseling, is typically around four to six months for the average couple. The process can take six to twelve months, or longer, for couples with severe, long-standing, or mental health issues. Usually it's not hard to decide when no more formal counseling is needed—everyone can see that the relationship is healing. Even friends and family can see the positive changes.

> Connectors may prefer to connect emotionally before becoming physically intimate while Achievers may go about it in the opposite direction.

Couples differ, and the actual course of therapy is highly variable. For some, therapy goes faster; for others, more slowly. Some become hung up in one phase or another. Sometimes prolonged individual work is required. Not all therapy succeeds in keeping spouses together. Sometimes one spouse decides they don't want to work to save the marriage and decides to drop out of counseling. A common expression of this is, "I love him, but I'm not *in love* with him. I'm ready to move on."

No one can force anyone to stay in a relationship. In simple terms, there are three main options: 1) divorce, 2) stay in an unhealthy and dysfunctional marriage, or 3) decide to change and seek any necessary help. The goal of therapy is to help both parties understand and choose the third option.

SELF-HELP

Maybe you recognize that you have a low-power marriage. Things could be better, but there is no crisis, major resentments, or detachment right now. And you want to work on your marriage. For whatever reason, you have decided that you want to try working through your issues without therapy. Depending on the nature of your marital issues, this may be a reasonable and viable alternative to formal counseling. Here are some things for you to consider.

One is to review the Self-Assessment—Marriage Essentials (chapter 2) together with your spouse. If you can't do it together, each of you could do it alone, then share your answers. Write out the answers and date the page. You may wish to do this over several sittings. It's okay if this assessment takes you several days; the main thing is to take this step very seriously.

Having completed the assessment, you and your mate should be able to prioritize areas from among the five where attention is needed first. Based on what you've learned about therapy, select some exercises or create your own exercises that focus on the priority areas.

If you're affiliated with a church or other house of worship, you may consider meeting with the pastor or other leader. If the pastor already knows you and is aware of your general circumstances, there may be less fear of sharing the details. Pastors may offer spiritual, faith-based ways to address your problems, directly incorporating your religious beliefs. Most pastors have training in counseling and will be able to provide guidance. They usually also recognize if the problems are beyond their level of expertise and can refer you to a mental health professional. A pastor can integrate psychological and spiritual resources to bring help, healing, hope, and wholeness to your life.

Some churches offer small groups, Bible studies, and/or life groups for couples or individuals that study topics that are particularly helpful for relationships. These groups typically include reading, reflection, and sharing among the members of the group or class. Members learn from the study materials and from each other. Perhaps some group members will have been through experiences similar to the one you're in at present.

Marriage retreats and weekend workshops, either secular or faith based, can be very helpful in improving your communication and conflict resolution abilities. They may also focus on forgiveness, trust building, and learning ways to be more intimately connected. Hope and encouragement come along with practical tools to build and grow a better relationship. For some couples, an intensive weekend experience provides just the boost they need to get their marriage back on track. As with small groups, hearing the true stories of other couples with similar experiences can be very comforting and provide new insights into your own situation.

> Hope and encouragement come along with practical tools to build and grow a better relationship.

If one partner has an addiction to drugs or alcohol, we recommend that the addiction be addressed as a priority. While formal rehabilitation, counseling, or therapy is the best option, many do get sober by seeking help from a twelve-step program like Alcoholics Anonymous (AA) or Narcotics Anonymous (NA). These programs provide principles and a course of action for recovery along with structure, support, accountability, and hope. Celebrate Recovery is a Christian program similar to AA/NA but is organized from the basis of biblical teaching and Christian theology.

SELF-ASSESSMENT—MARRIAGE ESSENTIALS

1. You are fully engaged, committed, and make the relationship with your spouse a priority.

   - Agree on regular "us" time to have relaxed conversation with no distractions at least several times a week. Make a written commitment to each other that your marriage is more important than work, hobbies, family, and friends.

- Identify together what issues are taking away time that you might otherwise spend together. Develop an action plan to free up more together time.

- Create individual and mutual goals that you'd like to achieve in your life together—for example a new job, having and raising children, taking a nice vacation, growing closer.

2. You participate as an equal partner in your marriage and take responsibility for (and only for) your own thoughts and actions.

    - Try to use only "I" statements.

    - Admit to your partner that you have not been the perfect spouse and be able to apologize.

    - Agree to stop all blaming, defensiveness, and justification.

    - Examine what your respective roles are. Consider switching for a while or sharing these. An example might be switching who does the dishes, takes out the trash, or pays the bills for three months.

    - Determine and share with your partner what you are going to work on changing in yourself.

3. You strive to communicate effectively and resolve conflict constructively.

    - Agree that you will always be willing to discuss areas of conflict, and use the seven-step approach.

    - Work on expressing yourself calmly no matter what the disagreement.

    - Think of how the other party will feel before you decide to speak.

- Speak in a way that attempts to minimize harsh feelings. Avoid fighting words, including "always" and "never." Use "and" instead of "but" when addressing concerns.

- Respect and appreciate each other's perspective, even when your opinions differ.

- Don't allow things to build inside.

- Celebrate success when you resolve a conflict well, even if you have to agree to disagree.

4. You are willing to forgive and work to build trust.

- Write a letter of forgiveness to yourself and to your spouse. Don't deliver it unless your spouse has agreed to accept it.

- Tell your partner that you are trying to trust him or her more.

- Do not use the silent treatment.

- Avoid bringing up the past; say what you need to say about present issues, constructively.

- Incorporate trust-building activities into your marriage.

5. You aim for physical and emotional intimacy.

- Spend fun time together—movies, other activities, or date nights are some ideas. Brainstorm about possibilities, then choose one and do it.

- Tell your partner how you experience emotional intimacy and what you would like from him or her.

- Schedule time for sex at least once a week when you will both be well-rested and happy.

- Give your partner a card at the end of the week expressing what you appreciated about him or her that week.

- Express affection and attention often, without having any other agenda. Go out on a date often. Take turns planning the date.

- Both partners should have an individual identity and spend time with same-sex friends.

After you've agreed on some concrete steps, try them for a month and then repeat the self-assessment. Compare your answers to your initial written report. Record your progress. Then repeat the cycle.

THE BOTTOM LINE:

- Tension, disagreement, and conflicts happen in all relationships. How the partners deal with them determines their net impact on the relationship. Resolving conflict and working through the associated feelings is essential to staying and growing close in marriage.
- The easy option in the short run is almost always the worst thing to do in the long run. Facing problems in a relationship makes things better. Avoiding them makes things worse.
- Marriage counseling or therapy is hard work in itself, but it will pay off if both parties are willing to do the work. Seek professional help in your relationship if you need it.

Conflict
occurs in all relationships.
How you handle it
determines its effect.

A Story of Victory

Winning the Love Fight

As you may recall, our characters Michael and Jessica had experienced a great deal of personal frustration and anger throughout their married life. That's the Love Fight. Feelings of anger and frustration are common for A/C couples, and Michael and Jessica didn't work through the issues to resolve these damaging emotions. Consequently, resentments built and detachment began. Jessica, figuring Michael would never change, busied herself with her business activities and the children. Michael worked more and more until eventually his work became his home. At that point, he crossed into self-destructive behavior by becoming involved with a woman who was not his wife.

Many Achievers become caught up in living a life in which their marriage seems to be just along for the ride and it gets little attention. Like so many others, Michael and Jessica didn't recognize how they were co-creating this deterioration in their relationship. When we left them, they had spent three days apart after Jessica uncovered Michael's extramarital affair. Jessica had blown up and Michael had taken off. Neither seemed to quite understand what had happened to their relationship. Now Michael was about to return home.

"WE NEED COUNSELING"

The air was chilly when Michael got home. At first neither had much to say to each other besides the obligatory hello. Eventually Jessica, who was hopeful about reconciling and saving the marriage, said, "We need counseling," which got no immediate response from Michael. But Jessica was not giving up so easily. She felt that they both had reasons to preserve their marriage. When Michael said nothing, she repeated, "We need counseling." Michael just stared, but seeing that she was about to say it again, he responded.

"I don't know what good it would do," he replied, reflecting his skepticism about therapy in general and his doubt about his own prospects with Jessica. He wasn't proud of his behavior, but he felt that Jessica had been ignoring him. Now that his infidelity was out in the open, he doubted that she would forgive him and instead would constantly hold the affair over his head. He felt that she'd never trust him again, and he also wasn't sure that he could get his feelings back for her.

> "People, perhaps unconsciously, often seem drawn to a life that's similar to what they experienced as children," he said. "It's what they know, and that may be comfortable, even though it may not be healthy for relationships."

Also, Michael wasn't at all disposed to digging into himself in therapy. It seemed easier somehow in his own mind to end the marriage and just move on with life. *It happens to a lot of people*, he had been thinking. From a practical standpoint, he was concerned about how all this would affect the boys and his bank account, but he was a little bit worried about winding up as an old man with a wife who cared only for her fitness center and her children. But, in reality, he wasn't sure yet what he wanted.

Jessica pressed on with her arguments about why they should work to save the marriage. Michael still wasn't buying it and Jessica began to cry. Michael, who didn't handle emotions well, particularly sadness and tears, did not know exactly what to do. But in order to stop the torrent of uncomfortable emotions, he finally agreed to go to marriage counseling. Jessica volunteered to make the arrangements.

Jessica called Dr. Matthew Tucker, the therapist recommended by her friend Susan, and scheduled individual appointments for herself and Michael. Susan said that Dr. Tucker had a direct, no-nonsense style, and Jessica thought Michael would listen more to a man than he would to a woman.

Jessica's Individual Visit

Dr. Tucker introduced himself, invited Jessica to sit down, and said, "What brings you here?" The floodgates opened. All of Jessica's emotions poured out in an anti-Michael rant. Michael's coolness, his workaholism, his adultery, lack of interest in her, and more came bursting out of Jessica, seemingly in a single breath.

After listening and validating her feelings, Dr. Tucker turned the conversation to her behavior, asking, "Tell me how *you've* contributed to these problems in your marriage." Naturally, Jessica was defensive, but Dr. Tucker explained, "Jessica, affairs typically don't happen in a vacuum. Usually affairs happen because of a combination of the individual's issues and underlying marital problems, and these marriage issues result from the behaviors of both partners. Nothing you did justifies Michael's actions, but we do need to talk about you and your behavior, too."

To her credit, Jessica was able to recognize that her focus on her business, fitness, family, and friends to the exclusion of Michael had helped to create some of the distance between them. Early in their marriage, she had tried to talk to Michael about issues, but he would either get angry or walk away. Eventually, Jessica had given up on conversation and redirected her energies into the boys, her friends, the fitness center, exercise, and community activities. She hadn't been good at praising or appreciating Michael's positive behaviors, either.

Dr. Tucker again assured Jessica that her behavior did not justify Michael's adultery, but that if she wanted to save the marriage, it would be important for her to understand and alter her own behavior. After all, it was the only thing she really could control.

She didn't confront Michael directly when she was hurt or angry, choosing instead to spend more time away from him and rebuff his attempts at physical intimacy. Jessica wasn't usually able to express her feelings constructively and effectively to Michael, and he didn't respond well at times when she did.

MICHAEL'S INDIVIDUAL VISIT

When Dr. Tucker asked Michael what had brought him here, Michael replied, "My wife wanted me to come." But with a little effort, Dr. Tucker soon had Michael talking more openly about the issues. Michael recounted his drifting away from Jessica, citing her inattention to him. He stressed that he had "worked hard to build a nice life for her," only to find that Jessica neglected him in favor of other people and activities.

> Each could see how to acknowledge the other's emotions and validate them, not necessarily agreeing, but at least not attacking their partner.

Basically, Michael spent the first portion of the visit defending his position and justifying his actions. In Michael's mind, working hard and being a good provider made him a good husband, which is what he had learned during his own childhood. Other than the affair, he had a hard time identifying ways he had contributed to the marital issues, and was convinced that Jessica was as much at fault as himself, even if she was blaming him exclusively. "Doctor, she has a pretty nice life. A lot of women would die for the kind of lifestyle I've provided, but she doesn't appreciate it or me," he said emphatically.

After twenty minutes, the conversation turned to Michael's childhood. After listening for a while, Dr. Tucker asked what Michael had learned from his dad about fatherhood and marriage. Michael replied, "Well, I'm not mean like he was. I try to be nice to Jessica and the kids. I'm doing much better than my father," which didn't really answer the question. So the counselor asked the question another way. "What did you learn, and how does it affect your relationships today?" Michael replied, "I guess I learned to work really hard."

At this point, Dr. Tucker validated Michael, while introducing the idea to Michael that he may have also learned some other lessons about relationships from his father—things like being a good provider is the way to show love, emotional issues and household chores are "women's work," and being critical and controlling are ways to motivate others.

By the end of the session, Michael admitted that it was possible that through the years he had not been meeting some of Jessica's legitimate emotional needs. He also acknowledged that his parents' marriage was dysfunctional and that his own marriage had similar problems. Michael's awareness of his own issues was still quite limited, but his mental window had opened a crack as a result of the conversation.

THE FIRST JOINT SESSION

The first session together was scheduled the week following the individual visits. It got off to a bad start when Michael arrived fifteen minutes late for the nine a.m. meeting due to a situation at work. Dr. Tucker replied, "Michael, what message are you sending when you arrive late to your first appointment together? Are you committed to therapy?"

Actually, Michael had been doing a lot of thinking about exactly those questions over the last week. He had decided that he really did want to save his marriage, but his difficulty with expressing emotions made it easy to be late for the actual emotional work of therapy. Surgical work was a lot easier and, of course, he was in charge in the hospital. Not so here. Michael recognized his own avoidant behavior. He apologized and agreed to commit to the therapy process.

That having been addressed, Dr. Tucker got right to the heart of the matter. "I believe you can work this out, if you want to," he began. "You will both need to change. The issues between you have been building for years, and it's going to take some work to overcome them. Each of you has, in your own way, lost your focus on your relationship and you've grown far apart. Poor communication and failure to resolve disagreements are the two main causes of your estrangement."

He went on, "Michael, you have not been emotionally open with Jessica or emotionally available to her. It's understandable, Michael, but you are emotionally underdeveloped and intellectually overdeveloped. Like many professionals, you aren't fully aware of your own feelings and emotional needs while having tremendous knowledge and command of facts. But in relationships, feelings are more important than facts."

"At the same time, Jessica, you have focused on Michael's faults and responded by withdrawing," he continued. "Neither of you is good at addressing difficult issues. Both of you prefer to avoid disagreeing and the accompanying emotions. Unfortunately, these unresolved conflicts remain inside you."

"The net result is that you are no longer intimate, physically or emotionally. Your trust in each other and your reliance on each other has faded as you've stopped sharing time together. You haven't been able to count on each other for quite a while, and Michael's affair was his way to escape from your relationship."

Jessica and Michael felt a little stung by the counselor's assessment but wanted to know more. Since their session time had been shortened due to Michael's tardiness, they decided to continue the discussion during a time slot that had opened up that same afternoon.

THE SECOND SESSION

That afternoon, as they talked, Jessica shared that she had realized that she experienced some of the same emotional reactions with Michael as she had had with her own father. She was sad, hurt, and angry when Michael was gone a lot at the hospital and was unable to constructively share her resulting emotions with

> Think of your relationship like a bank account. Every hurtful or negative interaction represents a withdrawal, and every positive interaction represents a deposit.

Michael. She had been helpless and powerless to change her father and felt abandoned when he left, but she had assumed that she could change Michael. Jessica's father was also unfaithful to her mother, and Jessica had wanted a different life.

But, like her mother after the abandonment, Jessica redirected her feelings into other people/activities and away from her marriage, which only created more distance and disconnection. Jessica decided, like her mother had, that her survival required her to take control of her own happiness, emotional connection, and support. Jessica responded by being more self-sufficient. She wasn't going to be completely caught off guard and without any financial resources like her mother, which was one reason she chose to purchase the fitness center. In addition, she took some of her unexpressed, unresolved anger and disappointment with her father and directed it toward Michael.

During this session, Jessica was able to see just how much energy she had put elsewhere, and she recognized that she was repeating a pattern that she had learned from her mother. She admitted that she felt she had lost her purpose when the children became more independent, and as a result had sought connection through her business, friendships, and activities.

Dr. Tucker explained that this was not uncommon. "People, perhaps unconsciously, often seem drawn to a life that's similar to what they experienced as children," he said. "It's what they know, and that may be comfortable, even though it may not be healthy for relationships."

Michael admitted that he did put work first, as his father had done, and found it difficult to be emotionally connected to anyone. He had been close to the boys when they were young but had also grown apart from them as they became teenagers and young adults. Dr. Tucker explained that this most likely related to Michael's apparent need to be in charge, which is easy with young kids but problematic as they grow older. "Many parents have difficulty maintaining a close relationship with their teenage children, but a controlling style like yours typically makes it a lot worse," the counselor said.

> Trust is the glue that binds together an intimate and meaningful relationship; without it, a marriage cannot survive.

Michael acknowledged that, although he did have fears and insecurities from time to time, he preferred to ignore them. He said he would never consider talking about them to anyone else, especially his wife. He believed that people are supposed to suck it up, grin and bear it, and just power through life's problems. As far as he was concerned, "Feelings aren't that important." "Feelings don't play any role in surgery," he said, to which Dr. Tucker replied, "Even if that's true, which I doubt, they certainly matter everywhere else."

Michael could see that because his own mother never challenged his father, he might have had a hard time being confronted and challenged by Jessica. As with Jessica, Michael had feelings of anger and hurt that he had been carrying from childhood. But, too often, he had directed this residual anger and hurt at Jessica. Yet, he had expected Jessica to fully accept him, even when his behavior was inappropriate and he became verbally abusive.

Before the end of the session, Michael agreed to discontinue all contact with the other woman and to focus exclusively on his marriage. Jessica agreed to cut back on outside activities and her business to focus on her marriage. Dr. Tucker suggested an initial therapy period of four months with a reassessment at the end of that time. Both Michael and Jessica agreed that saving the marriage would be the best option and both agreed to take responsibility for changing only themselves.

THE WORK STARTS

Dr. Tucker recommended that they begin by working on communication. Together they came up with the following action steps:

- As a couple, they agreed to schedule three twenty-minute communication sessions each week. Each session was to be seated, face-to-face, with no distractions, no interrupting, and a focus on deep connecting topics.
- They agreed to create a fun list of potentially mutually enjoyable activities and to initiate a weekly date night that would be on both of their calendars. When anything other than an extreme emergency threatened this time, they would each say that they had other plans already.

Dr. Tucker also asked each of them to create a pie chart diagram of the activities that consumed their average week—that is, what fraction of the 168 hours in a week was spent on work, sleeping, exercising, doing chores around the house, etc.

The counselor also suggested to Michael that he would benefit by broadening his identity. With a little effort, he could become more than just a hardworking, successful surgeon and husband. Essentially, he had all of his self-worth eggs in one basket—the "important doctor basket." By diversifying his life, pursuing new interests, and initiating some new male friendships, Michael would create ways to experience healthy connections with others. He would likely also experience more happiness, grow emotionally, and relate to Jessica better.

But for now, they agreed to work on communication and fun between just the two of them, which didn't go all that well at first. Their twenty-minute discussions were painful and strained. Their fun list sounded good, but neither could relax enough to really have any fun when they did go out.

They each called Dr. Tucker separately with concerns, but he advised each to keep at it until the next therapy session. And what a session that was! Michael and Jessica both came in hot from an argument that they'd just had the day before. Their son Jeff had called Jessica to tell her how homesick he was and how much he didn't like college. Clearly, he was struggling to adjust to his freshman year. While Jessica was discussing her concerns with Michael at their regular twenty-minute communication session, Michael wanted to stop talking about it when their scheduled time was up. Jessica blew her stack. "This is your son we're talking about! Try to care about him," she exclaimed, and it went downhill from there.

The same argument started up from where it left off almost immediately upon sitting down with Dr. Tucker. Jessica attacked Michael for "not caring about Jeff." Michael became angry, extremely defensive, and began to shout that "I do care, but I am just calmer about it than you!"

Basically, Michael attacked because he believed, as in sports and business, "the best defense is a good offense." He was hoping to shut down the conversation and make Jessica back off. Jessica was looking for him to instantly become a warmer, more caring person, but, of course, that wasn't happening. The more she pushed, the more he pushed back. In reality, neither liked to be told what to do.

They were caught up in blaming, defensiveness, and justification, rather than communication and problem solving. Despite the counselor's effort, neither could be redirected to a more productive discussion. All three were frustrated by the end of fifty minutes of arguing. At his request, they scheduled an early follow-up appointment.

THEY REGROUP

Dr. Tucker initiated the next meeting. "Let's discuss what happened at the last session and more about the dynamics of your relationship. I'll start," he said, in a serious but measured voice. "Neither of you is behaving as an adult toward the other. Michael, you are behaving as a rebellious and immature child. You insist on your way and throw a child-like temper tantrum when you don't get it." Before Michael could get a word out he went on, "Jessica, you aren't behaving as an adult either. Your scolding, nagging, and badgering are the signs of an overbearing parent who has lost her composure. Parent-child marriages often fail. It's time for both of you to choose adult behaviors. Adult discussions are more constructive and less painful."

> Intimacy comes in many forms, including physical, emotional, spiritual, recreational, and work intimacy.

He went on, "At our last session, neither of you was really listening to the other. Each of you was attacking. Neither was using 'I' statements. Both of you were inappropriate in your very negative and hurtful comments."

The counselor suggested Michael and Jessica apologize to each other for their behavior. And he coached them through statements of their feelings and apologies. Jessica started, "I get upset when you verbally attack me to shut down an emotional conversation." Michael replied, "I get angry when you assume I don't care and put words in my mouth."

"I'm sorry," Jessica replied. "Me too," Michael responded.

After this exchange, Dr. Tucker reviewed adult communication behaviors like listening, validation, assertiveness without aggressiveness, and taking time-outs if needed. Then he walked them through some scripted and unscripted role-playing focused on healthier ways of communicating. Both Michael and Jessica found this very helpful. Each could see how to acknowledge the other's emotions and validate them, not necessarily agreeing, but at least not attacking their partner. Michael and Jessica agreed to continue working to incorporate these strategies into their talks, both scheduled and unscheduled. Dr. Tucker stressed the usefulness of time-outs to allow people to avoid blowing up as emotions reach the boiling point. Time-outs provide each partner some time to gather his or her respective thoughts, manage the associated emotions, and respond in the best way he or she knows how.

> Physical and emotional intimacy are two problematic areas for most couples in trouble.

"This is important," he said, "because negative interactions like you're used to having—lashing out or shutting down—can destroy relationships. Think of your relationship like a bank account. Every hurtful or negative interaction represents a withdrawal, and every positive interaction represents a deposit. A big balance is a healthy relationship, and when the balance goes below zero, your account is closed. You two have been making some major withdrawals and very few deposits."

Dr. Tucker went on, "Given what I've seen so far, I think we should alter our original plan and try six months of therapy before reevaluating the situation. You each have individual issues to work on before much more work together will be productive. I'd like to see each of you separately for the next few sessions. Meanwhile, please continue to practice what we talked about today, and be sure to use the time-outs."

THE INDIVIDUAL SESSIONS

Michael's individual sessions focused on learning better interpersonal skills, including:

- Transitioning better from work to home. He learned to use breathing techniques, music, positive self-talk, and restructuring to change his mindset before arriving home.
- Becoming assertive instead of aggressive.

- Dialing down his critical and controlling personality traits.
- Increasing his emotional awareness, sensitivity to others, and expression of feelings.
- Trusting others more, increasing self-disclosure, and developing male friendships.

And, very importantly, Michael addressed unresolved childhood issues with his parents. He wrote two letters, one addressed to his mother and one to his father, in which he described the negative events and experiences that left him with unresolved shame, anger, and guilt. He shared his feelings, and forgave them.

> Dear Dad,
>
> I want to tell you about some things that happened in my childhood that still affect me today. I'm not blaming you or trying to make you feel guilty. Instead, my goal in writing this letter is to let go of negative emotions from the past that I've been holding on to. I hope that through this I can be a better husband and father, because these emotions from the past are hurting me in my relationships with my wife and children. And maybe I can even have a better relationship with you and we could be friends.
>
> Dad, I was intimidated by you and scared of you from my earliest memory. You got angry fast and often, and then yelled and cursed at Mom and me. I know you're an intense person. I am too, but you treated us badly. I didn't deserve it. No one deserved that.
>
> You provided us with material things and I appreciate it. I inherited your strong work ethic and it helped me become a successful surgeon like you.
>
> But you were hypercritical of everything that I did, and you wanted to control me. Nothing I did was ever good enough for

you. You never said "I love you" or even "good job." This hurt me in a big way, and I realize now that it gave me low self-esteem. I have always looked to others for praise, acceptance, and love. I found esteem through academics and eventually medicine. But I know now that I was substituting these achievements for the respect, admiration, and acceptance that I wanted from you.

I wish you had been more loving and more present for me. It hurt me that you weren't involved in my life like other kids' dads. It seemed that working and making money were more important to you than I was. I could never talk to you about any problems because you would either get upset or ignore me. I don't know which was worse. Unfortunately, I learned to shut out my feelings and withdraw from people.

I don't want to keep carrying my anger, resentment, hurt, and sadness. These emotions have caused me too many problems and I want to release them. I forgive you, Dad, for the things you did and said that hurt me and contributed to my anger. I forgive you for not being very involved in my life as a child and for not expressing your love and praise for me. I realize that you probably grew up much the same way and were repeating a pattern, like I was until now.

I choose to release all of my negative emotions and hope to have a better relationship with you and others as a result of letting go of the past. I love you and will try to express my love to you more consistently. I also plan to pass on to my children love, praise, acceptance, and approval since I now realize how important it is to a person's confidence and self-worth. Thank you, Dad, for the good things you gave me, including my drive and determination. Thank you also for allowing me to share my feelings with you.
Love, Michael

Michael read his letters in-session and participated in a role-play to assist with closure. These individual visits with Dr. Tucker helped Michael address some of his residual negative emotion, which he had directed toward Jessica and the boys, and gave him useful strategies to change his thoughts, actions, and emotions related to people.

> Blaming isn't helpful. What matters is commitment to change going forward.

Later he shared his letters with Jessica, which helped her understand him better and brought them closer together. Michael chose not to share them directly with his parents.

Jessica's individual work was focused primarily on taking responsibility only for herself and becoming more comfortable with conflict. She was learning to accept that others must make their own choices, and how to set appropriate limits and boundaries with others. In conflict, she learned to be assertive, rather than taking her usual passive-aggressive approach and soothing her feelings through exercise or socializing. Jessica practiced stating her points without belaboring them or building resentment if there was no immediate agreement.

To deal with issues related to her parents, Jessica used the same letter-writing technique as Michael had used. As Jessica began to build her self-esteem without relying on the invalid ideas she had internalized in childhood, she became less driven to acquire financial security, a large number of friendships, and perfect physical fitness. Gradually, she also became less concerned about the approval of others.

Only after this preparatory work was she ready to resolve the emotional pain related to her marriage, including Michael's affair. Now it was time to turn to forgiving Michael and to begin acknowledging his positive traits, accept that she couldn't change him, and respect him as an adult.

These changes took place over only three sessions for Jessica and six for Michael. Were Michael and Jessica completely emotionally healthy after these individual sessions? Far from it. But they had moved a little in the right direction, and often a little movement is all it takes to begin to build momentum and keep the improvement progressing.

RECOMMENDING JOINT SESSIONS

When they began meeting jointly again, they were still at the "improve communication" stage, which had been put on hold until the individual work sessions had been completed. Over the previous month, they had continued the scheduled twenty-minute sessions at home and the weekly date nights. It hadn't gone perfectly, but they had noticed some improvement.

In their first session back together, Dr. Tucker brought out the pie charts they'd each made weeks before. Reviewing them with each other, they realized anew just how little time they actually spent together and how far apart they'd grown. In fact, before entering therapy they'd had no dedicated time together other than time spent watching television.

Dr. Tucker asked them to begin to communicate directly about their needs, desires, and expectations. Like most couples, Michael and Jessica had very different individual desires, and like too many couples, each was focused mostly on getting his or her own needs met first without considering their partner's needs. This can be a delicate subject, but their communication with each other had improved enough to address this effectively with a third party present.

Michael desired more physical intimacy, time alone with Jessica, appreciation for his role as provider, and less nagging. Jessica, on the other hand, wanted more emotionally intimate conversations, more help managing the house, and more appreciation from Michael for her role in running the fitness center. Importantly, she also wanted Michael to continue to be faithful to her going forward, but she wasn't sure she could trust him.

Their assignment from Dr. Tucker was for each to select one of their spouse's desires and work on meeting it over the next few weeks— without telling the other what they were doing. Over the next few weeks, they made good progress. They actually had fun trying to figure out what desire their partner was working on meeting, and soon they each started working on more than one.

When they were communicating well enough, the counseling moved to the development of effective conflict resolution skills.

RESOLVING CONFLICT

The fact that Michael and Jessica couldn't constructively deal with conflict was one of the central issues that led to their marital crisis. Like many couples, not only couldn't they agree on the big issues, such as appropriate spending and parenting, they couldn't resolve the day-to-day little issues, either. They often chose to avoid disagreements altogether.

When they did discuss issues, the arguing typically and rapidly scaled up to the point that one or both of them would lash out and then at least one would detach. This pattern was quite predictable, which is why they often chose avoidance in the first place. Of course, the conflict wasn't over. Both parties had just gone silent, adding this issue onto the pile of unresolved conflict in their relationship.

Dr. Tucker guided them through discussion and resolution of two conflicts they selected. The first issue was only a couple of days old. Jessica had just come home from the sporting goods store with several shopping bags of clothes for herself and the boys and some equipment for the fitness center. Michael, immediately suspicious, rummaged through the bags to find the receipts. He saw that they added up to $600. He lit into her, "Jessica, what are you doing? How can you spend so much money on stuff we don't need?" Jessica shot back, "Come off it! Leave me alone! You bought that giant TV and surround sound equipment without a word to me about it! What did that cost us?" When Michael replied, "I'm the one who earns most of the money around here," Jessica simply left the room.

As they tried to get through the story together, they began to replay the actual argument with interruptions, angry voices, and biting comments.

Dr. Tucker jumped in, "Okay, perfect, let's work on this. Can we agree that the issue is spending a significant sum of money without the other's consent?" Both Michael and Jessica nodded.

Over the next fifteen minutes, they each expressed their anger, frustration, and resentment with the other about spending. And Dr. Tucker helped each to validate their partner's emotions. As they generated ideas, negotiated, and compromised, they decided to set an individual spending limit of $500. Purchases over that amount would require both to agree in advance.

Michael had the hardest time with this. Frankly, he was reluctant to compromise on any solution, but he did see the value for both of them in having some way to resolve the issue. The couple had an agreement that they could live with for the time being, and they were able to let go of any bad feelings.

Dr. Tucker asked them to try to use this process any time they felt there was even a minor disagreement between them, but regardless, to use it at least twice each week. Fortunately, over the next several weeks, the new method took hold and Jessica and Michael wound up using it more and more. Jessica reported that "Michael listens and doesn't blow up like he used to." Michael said that he found "Jessica is actually seeing it my way sometimes now. She doesn't sulk anymore."

FORGIVENESS

Forgiveness is often the toughest task in rebuilding a marriage or relationship.

For Michael and Jessica, their assignment was: "Each of you is to write two letters—one to your spouse and one to yourself," Dr. Tucker said. "Please write first about the actions of your spouse and events in your relationship that caused you to feel angry, hurt, sad, resentful, anxious, or guilty. Be sure to cover things that were done or said and also things that were not done or said, which have contributed to these strong feelings."

He continued, "In the second letter, write to yourself about your own actions and how they have harmed you and your relationship with your spouse. Include how you feel about that now and what specifically you intend to do in the future. In the last part of both letters, forgive these actions and inactions, release the associated feelings, and completely let go of the emotional pain. I know this is very hard," he added, "but it is essential to your continued progress. We all make mistakes, but what's important is changing our behavior going forward, which is much easier when we can forgive ourselves."

Michael had an especially hard time with his letters this time around. Although he was improving, emotional awareness and expression still were not natural for him. In his letter to Jessica, he struggled to capture his feelings, eventually listing anger, resentment, and disappointment. He was better able to outline the issues he had with Jessica—overinvolvement with the children and her business, excessive socializing, lack of physical intimacy, and "lack of respect for me as her husband." He expressed his forgiveness of Jessica, agreed to let go of the past, and to focus on the present and their future together.

In his letter to himself, Michael acknowledged his self-absorption as a major issue contributing to their marital problems. He identified his controlling and perfectionist nature, the childhood factors that had shaped his personality, and how he was perpetuating his damaging family legacy of hard work and no family life. He accepted responsibility for his actions, including the affair, expressed regret, and committed to change for the better. After finishing the letter, he apologized to Jessica again for his inappropriate and hurtful actions.

Jessica had a much easier time expressing her emotions and writing out her thoughts. She reported feeling anger, sadness, bitterness, frustration, shame, and resentment over the years, based on Michael's obsession with work, limited commitment to the family, lack of emotional intimacy, and his affair. However, she had great difficulty choosing to forgive Michael.

"He slept with her! How can I just let it go?" she asked Dr. Tucker during her emotional struggle.

Dr. Tucker explained that forgiveness was her choice. Michael had experienced his own emotional pain in the marriage, and he had apologized. "Michael has to deal with Michael. This is about you. Staying focused on judging him only keeps you from healing. Healing requires forgiveness, Jessica, and with time will free you of your pain," he said. Eventually she chose to forgive, agreeing to let go of her negative emotions and not bring it up again in the future.

Here is the letter Jessica wrote:

> Dear Michael,
>
> I know that forgiveness is letting go of my resentment and anger, and I want to do that. I want to stay married to you and to have a good marriage.
>
> How do I start? I wish I'd known that you were so dissatisfied.
>
> I guess I'll start at the beginning. I was so attracted to you! I loved your intelligence and your drive for success. It was clear to me that you were going places and I wanted to go with you. I knew that being a surgeon would mean you would work long hours, but I always thought things would get better. They never did!
>
> Many nights I'd sit home, sad and alone. Somewhere along the way, I started to get angry and resentful. I tried talking about it with you, but you didn't want to hear it and that just made me even more resentful. I feel that I supported you and your practice, but it wasn't good enough for you. I managed our home, too, but that wasn't to your standards either. Nothing I did was ever good enough.
>
> After our children were born, you were mad at me for giving them attention, and you said I took better care of

them than of you. That was probably true, but I needed them because you didn't have time for me.

I was hurt and humiliated by your criticism. I spent more time working out with friends and running the fitness center to feel good, but that only made you more critical and controlling. Your treatment has humiliated me in front of my friends. How come you could never talk with me about issues? Instead, you chose to lecture me or talk about me with others.

I'm disgusted by your affair. Yes, I guess I knew our relationship wasn't good, but I didn't stray. I'm also hurt, angry, sad, and ashamed over this whole thing. I have no respect for you right now, and am going to have a difficult time ever trusting you again. Did you ever even think about how this would hurt me?

Michael, I thought you were a man of integrity, honesty, and faithfulness. I accepted that you were a little socially immature—yes, but sneaky and devious—no. But was I ever wrong about that.

There, I've expressed myself like Dr. Tucker suggested, but I realize that if we are going to stay together I have to forgive you and work on trusting you again. I'm ready to do that. I want to forgive you for your unfaithfulness and I know that we've been neglecting our marriage for a long time. I am letting go of my pain, my anger, hurt, and sadness.

I also realize that I have some growing to do, that the more comfortable and secure I am with myself, the easier it will be for me to forgive you. I want to trust you again, but I think it will take a long time. Try to understand that and not force me.

Michael, I still love you. I want to be excited about you, like I was at first, and I want you to be excited about me. So, I choose to forgive you for the affairs, the long hours at work, the criticism, the emotional distance, and your avoidance of our family life. This is not easy for me, but I am working on understanding and being more responsive to your needs. I want a happy marriage with you. I will pay attention to our marriage and won't rehash our past. I am letting go of the pain.

Love, Jessica

As with Michael, Jessica's second letter proved that she had gained insight into her own self-centeredness, conflict avoidance, and passive-aggressiveness. She also recognized how she had learned these traits growing up as she did, and admitted how these had damaged her relationship with Michael. She apologized to Michael for shifting her time and focus to the children, her business, and her friendships when he wouldn't modify his behaviors, and for accepting a detached and passionless marriage. In addition, she forgave herself and committed to positive change.

> **Suffering and Healing Often Occur Together**
> We make our problems worse by failing to face them. We do this because, at the time, it seems less painful than confronting and working through our relationship issues. Yet, it's only in facing our issues squarely that we can grow and heal. When we work through the pain, we become better for it. Face the pain, and life gets better.

It was an emotional couple of sessions when they read the letters aloud to each other. Michael cried when he read his letters, and Jessica cried during all the letters. All three sat quietly for some time after they were finished. In the silence, it was clear that things were now very different than they had been just a few moments before.

BUILDING TRUST

Several sessions had passed since the "letter sessions," and Dr. Tucker felt that therapy was proceeding well enough to reduce the frequency of sessions from weekly to twice a month. All told, Michael and Jessica had been in counseling six months now. The counselor told them, "You are now firmly on the right course. All you need to do is be serious and continue the process."

With the solid foundation of communication, conflict resolution, and forgiveness in place, it was time to build trust. Trust is the glue that binds together an intimate and meaningful relationship; without it, a marriage cannot survive. But trust can't be conjured up out of thin air or bought at the corner grocery store. Trust builds gradually over time through consistency in words and deeds. Trust is earned one day at a time, but it can be destroyed in a moment.

The communication exercises Jessica and Michael had put into practice had been helping to create some trust all along. But it could only go so far, because communication, forgiveness, and trust are so closely intertwined. Communicating and conflict resolution are easier when the parties trust each other. Forgiveness is hard without trust, but trust is hard without forgiveness.

Trust can be rebuilt over time by being completely honest with each other and taking actions completely aligned with one's words. Jessica's biggest fear continued to be that Michael would be unfaithful again. Michael agreed to be forthcoming about his activities outside the house and to allow Jessica unrestricted access to his e-mail, social media accounts, and cell phone. And he followed through on these commitments. After four months or so, Jessica didn't feel a need to ask as many questions or closely monitor Michael's behaviors.

During this period, Michael and Jessica were communicating more consistently, and routinely working through conflict. They were starting to enjoy the date nights together. Jessica gradually accepted that, although she could never control Michael's behavior, she could choose to trust him or to be suspicious. Michael had proven to be trustworthy, and Jessica had realized that strengthening the bond between them was much more important than monitoring Michael. Their hard work was paying off. She moved to a deeper level of forgiveness and a better focus on the present.

Describing the changes they were seeing in their relationship and in each other, Jessica said, "Things are changing. Michael is much more open and less critical. He's apologized to me a lot, sometimes even when I wasn't looking for an apology. It's hard to believe how much progress we've made."

Michael agreed. He said, "Jessica is more concerned about me now. She listens to me and cares about how I'm doing."

DEVELOPING INTIMACY

Finally, it was time to focus more on achieving true emotional and physical intimacy. Michael and Jessica were quite wary, but they had learned throughout the process of therapy to try to understand and accommodate their partner's uniqueness. Part of marriage or any close relationship is the ability to be flexible. This can be a little bit tricky. In the give-and-take of marriage, sometimes you are the giver and at other times you are the recipient. It's important to keep things relatively balanced, but just as important not to keep score.

Intimacy comes in many forms, including physical, emotional, spiritual, recreational, and work intimacy. Physical and emotional intimacy are two problematic areas for most couples in trouble. Michael and Jessica shared little emotional intimacy between them before beginning therapy. Their conversations were largely logistical in nature and void of most emotion, except frustration and anger. Without this emotional connection, their sexual relationship withered and died. This only reinforced the emotional distance, and they grew further and further apart.

Jessica continued to have reservations about sex with Michael. She felt that Michael had been unfaithful because he needed someone "more sexy and prettier." She was insecure about her own attractiveness and sex appeal.

The reality was that Michael had decided to sleep with another woman only because she was so interested in him at the time. It all seemed so much easier than working on his own marriage. This new woman had been encouraging, admiring, and understanding in ways that Jessica was not at the time. Of course, Michael's relationship with his mistress wasn't nearly as complicated as a marriage—no living together and running a household, raising children, or struggling with other mutual responsibilities. It was all excitement, with no routine.

And Michael, the driven high-achiever, had been asking, "What's next for me?" Having accomplished his professional goals, he was restless for a new challenge. So Michael's infidelity was never a direct rejection of Jessica. Their lack of connection, combined with his emotional issues and easy opportunity, left him vulnerable.

Dr. Tucker worked with them on ways to recommence a physical relationship gradually. Michael understood it wasn't all about the sex, and they developed a plan for hand-holding, backrubs, and hugs, in addition to sex. This physical affection short of sex really seemed to help them a lot in this regard. Jessica did want to re-engage physically, and once she could trust Michael and understand that he still did desire her, she was able to relax and desire him as well.

CONCLUSION

At the end of a year, Dr. Tucker felt Jessica and Michael were ready to be on their own. The changes in their relationship were obvious. In his office, Michael and Jessica sat on the couch together, and Michael had his hand on Jessica's leg. They spoke with respect and affection for each other, and smiled when they talked.

In therapy, they had committed to the process and had done the work, despite their initial skepticism. In fact, at the beginning, neither believed that their spouse would change, and each had privately consulted a divorce attorney. Yet they stuck with the process and each came to understand himself/herself and their spouse as a unique individual with positives and negatives. By accepting their individuality—warts and all—and taking action to improve themselves and improve the marriage, they did just that. They each became a better spouse, a better parent, and a better person.

Believe it, therapy works if you actually do the work of therapy.

THE BOTTOM LINE:

- Blaming isn't helpful. What matters is commitment to change going forward. When you are committed to changing yourself and willing to release any defensiveness and justification, you can create healthy and happy relationships.
- Therapy does work. With counseling, most marriages survive major problems, even infidelity, but the partners have to want to do the work.
- Have the courage to seek the help you need. Prioritize relationships and realize that intimacy is an essential part of our human existence. Make a life as well as a living.

Don't get so busy *making a living* that you forget *to make a life.*

A Story of Defeat

Losing by Power Failure

Happy endings are always nice. But it doesn't always happen like that. Sometimes one partner isn't willing to continue doing the work and the marriage fails. In this Power Failure situation, that partner is usually the "powerful" one. Nevertheless, healing can happen for the spouse who chooses to continue the hard work of therapy. Reality being what it is, therefore, an alternate ending is possible for Michael and Jessica. This version picks up the story after Michael has reluctantly agreed to see Dr. Tucker and the couple are at their second session together.

THE SECOND SESSION

The next week didn't start well as Michael arrived ten minutes late for the appointment. Dr. Tucker called him on it and Michael made a work-related excuse. Things went downhill from there as they began to review the results of the past week's listening assignment and Michael revealed that he hadn't read the article or thought about it at all. "I was too busy reading medical articles and taking care of patients," he said.

Jessica started shouting, but Dr. Tucker interrupted and asked for calm. After Jessica had cooled down, Dr. Tucker spoke again. "Michael," he said, "therapy requires commitment. It takes work. Are you committed and motivated to heal your marriage? Your relationship can be improved, but you have to make the effort. Will you commit to doing the work?"

Actually, Michael had been doing a lot of thinking about that over the last week. He was convinced that he was right and that he would be happier with someone else. He was ready to move on "to find a woman who appreciates me." In his mind, that woman was the nurse with whom he was still having an affair. Mentally he was already checked out of his marriage and was looking for an opportunity to make a break and blame Jessica. Dr. Tucker's inquiry was his cue. "No," he said. "I'm tired of being put down and not being appreciated. I don't want to waste any more time or money talking about it." He stood up and walked out, closing the door behind him.

After Michael walked out, Jessica sat there in shock and began to weep. She couldn't believe that her marriage of twenty-two years was over that quickly. Michael was gone.

JESSICA'S THERAPY

Jessica wanted to continue therapy on her own, but if it was going to be just about her, she wanted to see a woman. Dr. Tucker recommended Dr. Amanda Wilson. In the weeks that followed, Jessica was a complicated bundle of nerves. Anger, sadness, hurt, resentment, guilt, and fear came and went, and mixed together—so much so that she didn't always know what she was feeling. She just knew that she felt bad. Her new therapist helped her through the grieving process and dealing with the added stress of divorce proceedings. She encouraged her to start journaling her feelings as a means of sorting through and releasing them.

> Jessica learned to modify her thinking and manage her emotions.

With her therapist's help, Jessica learned to modify her thinking and manage her emotions. By replacing negative and critical self-talk with more realistic thinking, she felt a little better. Used to blaming herself, Jessica learned to avoid overpersonalization and accept that "the relationship failed," as opposed to "I failed." Incorporating relaxation techniques at the same time, such as deep, slow abdominal breathing, helped even more. As she modified her thoughts and actions, her emotions were not as overwhelming and more manageable.

Jessica also worked on living in the present, taking life just one day at a time. Dr. Wilson explained, "Think about driving. The small rearview mirror allows you to see where you've been; that's your car's past." She went on, "Through the windshield you see your car's future—where you're going. But you can only see so far. You can't see miles and miles or around corners, yet you drive just fine taking the journey one view at a time. So live like that, Jessica. Just as you only glance at the rearview mirror occasionally while driving, don't get stuck in the past in your life—with all its guilt, regret, and resentment. And as you focus on the view through the windshield while driving, focus on living your life now without imagining the road you can't yet see and becoming fearful and anxious." Jessica could envision what the counselor was talking about.

Dr. Wilson also recommended that Jessica continue working, exercise, and avoid alcohol during this stressful time. In addition to her regular workout routine, Jessica began daily walks with her friend Susan. Walking and talking with Susan proved to be very helpful, as Susan had been through something very similar herself. Dr. Wilson and Susan also encouraged Jessica to join a Divorce Recovery Group to learn more about the divorce process and relate to others who understood it by experience.

Jessica made relatively quick progress in therapy. She was motivated and committed to changing herself. She took notes every session, completed all of her homework, and made every effort to incorporate the things she was learning. It got easier for her as she noticed how much better she felt when using her new skills and how people seemed to respond to her differently as well.

Gradually, Jessica was better able to focus on understanding exactly why and how the marriage failed. Naturally, she wanted to blame Michael, and she did. But she finally accepted that she couldn't change Michael and needed to focus solely on understanding and changing her own thoughts, emotions, and behavior. Jessica also wanted to learn about her role in the demise of her marriage so that she wouldn't repeat the pattern. Dr. Wilson helped her see how her energy had been channeled to the fitness center, friendships, and her children.

As Jessica gained insight into herself, she recognized that she was attracted to a certain type of man—intelligent, driven, and successful. Though Michael was still a resident when they had met, Jessica had spotted a winner. But she didn't spot his warning signs—emotional detachment and high need for control. Now she was more in tune with the larger picture.

Jessica was able to accept that she wasn't perfect either. She had avoided conflict, feared rejection, and wasn't able to effectively engage Michael. Her communication style was passive-aggressive, indirect, and nagging in nature. It didn't work, but she never tried a different approach. In the end, she had immersed herself in the fitness center, the children, and her friends and tuned Michael out. She received more rewards and reinforcement from those than she ever did from her husband. Exercise, work, and socialization had filled some of the emotional void, as she became less connected with Michael.

Dr. Wilson helped Jessica see that communicating assertively, directly, and constructively would be one of the most important changes she could make. "Jessica, communicating assertively simply means expressing your feelings as it relates to the other person's behavior," she said. "An example is, 'I feel frustrated when you fall asleep while I'm talking to you.' Using 'I' instead of 'you' prevents the statements from being seen as a personal attack. So this is not criticism, but rather a direct expression of feelings." She added, "Remember, your goal is not to change the other person's behavior, just to express your feelings. Being assertive will raise your self-esteem and self-respect."

Like so many people in this situation, Jessica's self-esteem was low and almost completely based on externals. She had never had a significant internal sense of self-worth. For most of her life, fear and guilt were her primary motivators. She wanted everyone to be happy and often placed others' needs above her own. Praise and approval from others, social connection, physical fitness, and popularity were the measures of her value to herself. This focus on the externals and "what others think" led to a lot of fear, frustration, and disappointment over the years. She learned that self-esteem was an inside job, and focused her efforts on self-acceptance, forgiveness, saying no consistently, incorporating healthy boundaries, and nurturing her faith and friendships.

> **Self-Esteem Is an Inside Job**
> Who determines your self-esteem? Do you let your spouse, family, coworkers, or neighbors decide if you're a valuable person? Maybe you learned that as a child. It's time to learn something new. You can decide to value yourself simply for being yourself. The opinions of others don't have to matter to you. You get to choose if they do or not. You can accept, praise, love, and forgive yourself regardless of others' opinions. Love yourself unconditionally.

Together Dr. Wilson and Jessica identified the traits she wanted to change—conflict avoidance, passive-aggressiveness, insecurity, and people pleasing—all of which are rooted in fear. Jessica feared failure, conflict, disapproval, rejection, and abandonment.

MORE WORK

Over several months, Jessica worked hard. Through in-session exercises and role-playing, and out-of-session homework, Jessica learned to accept, praise, and forgive herself. She improved at putting herself first, communicating directly and assertively, and worrying less about what "everyone thinks of me."

She continued walking and talking with Susan, but no longer every day. And now the conversation wasn't all about her anymore. One day she realized how much good was coming from therapy. Yes, it was quite painful, but the more she improved, the more she could see why this was so important. She told Susan, "I love who I am becoming. I didn't know I could be this person. It feels good." Jessica was finding herself and establishing an identity of her own. Her self-worth was no longer contingent upon others or things; instead, it was based on internal strengths and choices. Along the way, Jessica decided not to date, although some men had asked her out. She knew completing therapy before pursuing another relationship would help her avoid the same mistakes. Despite her personal progress, Jessica felt tremendous guilt and fear about how her marriage and the divorce would affect her children. She wanted them to find happiness in marriage and felt that she and Michael had not been good role models. Jessica didn't want them to think that a healthy marriage looked like the one she had had with their dad. Jessica also wanted to be sure that her sons didn't blame themselves for their parents' failed marriage.

Dr. Wilson encouraged Jessica to share these concerns with her sons, listen to their reactions, validate their feelings, and answer their questions. She did, and everyone felt better about the future together. This set the stage for more conversations about relationship issues with her. Eventually she was able to help the boys understand the components of a healthy relationship and how to recognize red flags.

When Jessica seemed ready, her therapist suggested that she write three letters—one to her mother, one to her father, and one to herself.

To her mother, Jessica described her frustration, anger, and disappointment at repeating the same caretaking pattern with Michael that her mother had modeled with her father. Next, she covered her resentment for being treated differently from her brothers, and for the conditional love she had felt from her parents. Jessica had been expected to pick up the slack for her brothers and assume responsibilities not required of them. "You only loved me when I was the 'good girl,' and you made sure I knew it," she wrote. Jessica concluded the letter by forgiving and letting go of the loneliness, resentment, and pain she had been holding for so many years.

Jessica's intensity increased when writing to her father. Her internal need for his approval had never ended. Even as an adult, she was still trying to please him, only to be disappointed and hurt by his lack of responsiveness. With the letter, she acknowledged that even if he wasn't changing, she was going to be different and let go of her pain. It took two evenings and a whole box of tissues to get all six pages out. Here's a small excerpt:

> . . . You were gone a lot when I was growing up, and you didn't spend any time with me when you were home. I was just a girl, not nearly as important as your sons. You expected me to keep house, like Mom, and to be seen and not heard. This crushed me and made me feel worthless. Why did you leave us? I was expected to pick up the pieces when you left, and you never accepted any responsibility for abandoning us. I can't believe I still wanted your approval . . . even to the point of marrying someone who was emotionally unavailable like you with the hopes of making him change.
>
> I wanted you to love me, but you kept your distance. You rejected me. I tried and tried to win your approval. Here I am as an adult still trying to win it. You hurt me badly. I'm still hurting. This sucks . . .

Jessica surprised herself by the depth of the feelings and the sheer number of negative experiences she remembered. No wonder I've got

206 | THE LOVE FIGHT

problems, she thought. In the end, she chose to forgive her father and let go of the past hurts and emotional pain, which she expressed as follows:

> It is time for me to forgive you for the ways you hurt me. I'm choosing to let go of the negative emotions from the past and release the pain. I realize that your childhood was dysfunctional too, and you didn't get love and affection from your parents. I forgive you, Dad, and will no longer hang on to my bad feelings toward you. I am worthy of love and no longer need your approval or acceptance in order to feel good about myself.

After reading the letter in-session, she and Dr. Wilson acted it out. Dr. Wilson played her father, and Jessica played herself. As her "father," Dr. Wilson apologized and talked about "his" own emotional issues. "I'm sorry, Jessica," she started. "I wasn't the father that you needed. I myself experienced very little love growing up and I guess I repeated that with you." She added, "Although I never told you directly, Jessica, I'm very proud of you. I'm sorry that I spent so much time on business and missed out on a close relationship with you and our family." This role-playing exercise helped Jessica achieve a sense of acceptance and closure for the hurts that had troubled her as long as she could remember.

A New Viewpoint Creates New Views

Perhaps you've seen the drawing that looks like either a young woman or an old woman depending on just how you look at it. A lot of life is like that too. Changing the way you look at things changes the way things look. As with the optical illusion, it's not always easy to do. One of the major roles of a therapist is to help you see things differently. When you see things differently, your reactions and responses can change for the better. Be open to a new viewpoint.

Jessica now could see more of the connection between her childhood and her marriage. She had been subconsciously working through the emotional pain of her father's distance with her distant husband! By letting go of the hurt from both relationships, she could relax, become more trusting, and not anticipate rejection or bring unresolved anger into her next relationship.

After this, her letter to herself came more easily. She was able to acknowledge the mistakes she had made, since she was already growing into a new person and seeing a lot of those issues as behind her. Jessica forgave herself. She forgave herself for ignoring the red flags early on in the marriage and for detaching from Michael and "checking out" and redirecting her energies into her business and friendships when it appeared nothing would change. Jessica wished that she had pushed for counseling years earlier, knowing that even if Michael had refused, she could have gotten help alone. In the end, Jessica forgave herself completely and accepted that the past was past.

FINISHING UP

All told, when Jessica had been through six months of therapy, she was doing really great. Dr. Wilson recommended that the last few months be devoted to launching Jessica's new life. She continued to develop better interpersonal skills and ways to have healthier relationships with everyone.

Jessica learned to set better boundaries, since her old pattern had been to agree to things she didn't want to do or didn't have time for. She became more selective in how she spent her time and with whom she spent it. She practiced addressing conflict head-on and openly sharing negative feelings. Jessica also improved on listening to others and letting them express themselves.

She scaled back her need to nurture everyone, and practiced accepting the generosity of others. Jessica began to delegate tasks and ask for help from others. Previously, she had been only comfortable as a giver rather than as a receiver. She was able to accept compliments now without negating them and found it easier to allow others to do nice things for her. As Jessica changed, she felt more in control of her life, and she felt empowered by her self-accepting attitude. She didn't worry as much about what others thought of her and realized that what she thought of herself mattered the most.

Dr. Wilson encouraged her to try slowing down and not always doing everything for others like she had in the past. She helped Jessica identify the many positive qualities she possessed. In the end, Jessica allowed herself to be human and shared more flaws and inadequacies with others. She found that people felt more comfortable around her since they didn't have to compete with her perfectionism. Jessica liked the person that she had become and didn't need to spend time trying to convince others of her worthiness.

Conclusion

People can heal. You can be well inside. Jessica did far better than simply survive. Sure, it would have been nice if Michael had stayed and worked on himself, but he wasn't willing. No one could compel Michael to change. But Jessica did change herself and grew emotionally, to the point where she is far less likely to repeat the painful patterns of her past.

As for Michael, people like him often find new partners, perhaps thinking, "It will be different this time." But usually it isn't that different. Conflicts happen. Marriages end. Sometimes there are more than two or three spouses before the "Michaels" of our world wake up to their own shortcomings. Sometimes they never do.

THE BOTTOM LINE:

- Ultimately having a good relationship depends on you, and you are responsible for your emotional development, regardless of what your partner chooses to do or not do.
- Change is painful, but inaction makes problems worse. Many people repeat cycles of dysfunctional relationships before they come to see that they can change to create better relationships.
- Accepting the situation and your own issues starts the healing process. After that, positive changes happen from the inside out.
- Emotionally healthy people attract other emotionally healthy people, and the reverse is true as well. If you want to participate in successful relationships, strive for emotional maturity yourself.

Sometimes you must let go of what *you have* in order to find what *you need.*

Join the Fight!

Trading a Good Lifestyle for a Good Life

What you've read to this point has been about the experiences of others. But this chapter is about you.

Perhaps you're an Achiever in a Power Failure situation thinking about greener pastures. Or you could be a Connector in an emotionally remote, "low power" relationship. Maybe you've already had a divorce or have failed in other relationships. Have you wondered why you've had or are having so many relationship problems? It is well worth the time to slow down a little and examine your life and yourself. If you don't, your relationship issues may multiply.

Many high-powered professionals run into problems at the pinnacle of their career, often around ages forty-five to fifty-five. The drive to climb the ladder has abated or there are no other rungs left. The children have moved out, business is functioning well, and life seems reasonably stable. And the Achiever is wondering what's next. Without a major challenge, Achievers may, even unconsciously, create their own chaos. Uncomfortable emotions that have been ignored or denied through busyness may begin to surface. And while their minds are hyperactive, their bodies are letting them know their age. The resultant mind-body power struggle can create other, new uncomfortable feelings for which the Achiever may be unprepared.

Connectors in midlife may also feel that something is missing. With the children grown and the nest empty, how is the marriage? Possibly not so good. Maybe what's missing is emotional closeness with his or her Achiever spouse. The Connector may feel that the marriage has seemingly slipped away over the years. They may experience sadness, anxiety, or frustration and be unsure just what to do now.

This is fertile territory for either emotional growth or for dysfunctional and relationship-destroying behavior. You've made it here, but where are you going? Are you convinced yet that change is necessary—that you've had enough of the drama? Or maybe you want a more fulfilling life, a life of happiness and meaning, and realize now that you can have it. You recognize that a good *lifestyle* doesn't represent a good *life*.

It's never too late to change. If you are married or want to be, you *can* be in a deep, satisfying, and fulfilling relationship with your spouse. A healthy marriage can be one of the best parts of life. Studies show that married people live longer and are in better physical and emotional health. Marriage can be particularly good for high-powered men. Married men earn more money, have greater social support, and have sex more than similarly situated unmarried men.[1]

> In any relationship the individuals are always either growing closer together or moving farther apart. There is no standing still.

MARRIAGE TAKES EFFORT

Maybe there is such a thing as love at first sight, but there's a lot of life to live after that first sight.

Few people truly understand what they are getting into when they get married. How could they? People often select mates that complement them or make up for their emotional weaknesses. It's only natural.

However, when individuals don't grow but become dependent on their partner to make up for their deficiencies, they're headed for trouble. One may be better at socializing, expressing feelings, and being organized, and one may be better at being assertive, making decisions, and setting boundaries. Sometimes it takes a crisis to recognize and address the dynamics. Complementing each other is fine, as long as each partner continues to learn, grow, and accept adult responsibilities.

Often problems start when "life happens" and the relationship is stressed by adversity, big or small. When a good foundation is present, hard times can help spouses grow closer. But too often the foundation was never well constructed or is now crumbling beneath the relationship it's supposed to be supporting. Marriage is about working together and sharing the burdens along with the celebrations.

A foundational weakness might be a deficit in important relationship skills, such as communication and conflict resolution. Or it might be that one or both partners' priorities are wrong and they choose things or activities over people. Some individuals try to justify themselves by blaming the other. This is an attempt to avoid their own responsibility and need for change. Most often, a combination of factors results in a loss of focus, drifting apart, and an eventual crisis. These differences, and a lack of knowledge about how to manage them, may prevent a couple from growing closer when "life happens."

While adversity may shine a piercing light on a couple's relational weaknesses, *in any relationship* the individuals are always either growing closer together or moving farther apart. There is no standing still. The main factors determining which of these occurs are the emotional health of the partners and their desire to invest in the relationship. Of course, these things go together—the more emotionally healthy partners are usually more committed to working on the relationship. To enhance your relationships, make a commitment to them, and commit to improving your own emotional health.

On the other hand, many individuals become stuck and can't break free by themselves. This is where a qualified professional can help. Do not be afraid to seek professional help at the first sign that you're not able to effectively create a closer relationship on your own. Seeking help is a sign of strength, not weakness. The sooner you seek help, the greater the chances are that the two of you will achieve the healthy, satisfying relationship that you desire.

Just as an injured athlete benefits from physical therapy to get back in the game, couples with emotional injuries benefit from marital therapy to develop healthy relationships. Of course, overachieving athletes may deny their injury and play through the pain in order to compete, which typically worsens the problem. Likewise, couples may ignore, deny, and compartmentalize their emotional pain, which leads to further relationship problems down the road of life.

Quite commonly, those who refuse help or deny the need for help are typically the ones that need it the most. It's hard to admit that you have a problem, much less that you are part of the problem and need to be part of the solution. This is especially difficult for high-powered professional types. Security and pride in their career may mask insecurity and weakness in their marriage or interpersonal relationships.

> Just as an injured athlete benefits from physical therapy to get back in the game, couples with emotional injuries benefit from marital therapy to develop healthy relationships.

But emotional pain and conflict don't go away on their own. Ignoring these issues makes the problems worse, eventually. If insanity is doing the same thing over and over again while expecting a different outcome, then be prepared to do something different.

Couples can and do work through major problems to heal, forgive, trust, and deepen their marital bonds. Infidelity doesn't have to cause divorce. In fact, most marriages do survive an affair. Researchers Tashman and Dougherty found that only 20–25 percent of divorces are caused by infidelity, and 70–80 percent of couples stay together after the affair is over.[2]

Therapy can help, if you will do the work. Marriages do get healthier and happier, and most people who have divorced would advise others to stay and work it out.[3] Such positive changes don't happen overnight. They require the commitment and effort of *both* partners. But those who take responsibility for changing themselves do make it work.

MARRIAGE TAKES UNDIVIDED ATTENTION

It's difficult, if not impossible, to invest in your marriage if you're distracted. And there are so many distractions in life—work, hobbies, events, media, and technology. Life comes at you fast. Relationships take time. Keep your focus and make the time.

Paradoxically, the "good times" may be when your relationships are most vulnerable. When the money's good and you're on top of the world, you can lose your focus on what's really important.

Being smart certainly offers no guarantee of marriage protection. Many very smart people make very destructive choices—sometimes over and over again. It's not uncommon for highly intelligent people to have a difficult time relating to others. Although great at thinking, they're not so great at feeling, and remember that emotions connect people. Relationships have little to do with intellectual intelligence and everything to do with emotional intelligence, and you can increase the latter.

Keeping your focus on relationships may require you to live differently from others around you—at home, at church, or at work. You may even be seen as countercultural, declining a promotion at the office to spend more time with your family. That's okay. Many Achievers don't seem to be growing their emotional health and improving their relationships. They haven't made it a focus and may never make it a priority—unless and until they experience an emotional or relationship crisis. Even then, they may not be willing to change. Prioritize your marriage. Agree on some mutual goals with your spouse. What do you want out of your life together? How can the two of you create the results you want by working together? How will you know you're on track? How will you celebrate your successes?

Identify people you admire for their character, emotional maturity, and loving relationships with family and friends. Ask them how they do it. What lessons could you apply to your own life?

It's important to have at least a few trustworthy friends with whom you can just be yourself. Your true friends will help support you in hard times and hold you accountable in good times. Staying connected to healthy people will keep you grounded and growing.

YOU MAY NEED TO CHANGE

Situations that create cracks in relationships and may result in deep divides are going to happen in your life. You cannot avoid such stress, but you can choose how you react to it. Most people don't think about choosing, they just react by instinct—usually with old behavior they learned long ago.

These instinctive reactions are like an old baseball mitt. It's familiar, broken in, very comfortable, and fits your hand just right. Unfortunately, it's also worn out with torn webbing and no padding, and it's just not very good for catching the ball. New behaviors are like a new mitt—more effective, but uncomfortable at first. With some breaking in, it will work great.

A typical old response is attempting to get things under control, but this controlling response can be damaging to relationships. Remember that control is the single most harmful characteristic for any relationship.

Throwing yourself into your job or other activities in order to avoid dealing with the issues is another common "old response." This doesn't usually work either.

So, you may need to learn new ideas, new ways of thinking, and new patterns of behavior. Everyone has issues from their past that affect their current relationships. Maybe they're minor or maybe not. Perhaps suppressed feelings from long ago burst out in your emotional reactions today. Are you using any adaptive coping skills from your childhood that are maladaptive as an adult? Has conditional love or emotional abuse from the past created an obsession with proving your worth and value through achievement?

> **Are You Living to Die or Dying to Live?**
> Are you just "marking time" in life? Are you observing your life more than living it? If so, don't expect too much out of life. To get more out of life you've got to put more into it. Start with your relationships. As you feel the difference, you'll be energized to do even more. Get the passion back. Make life count.

Your childhood experiences and personality development don't have to determine your future success in your relationships. You don't have to repeat the patterns of those who raised you. You can choose to move beyond your past. Reflect on what behavior is good for the relationship before acting out old patterns. Now is the time to let go of the past and create a new future. Choose to release the pain. Decide how you want to live the rest of your life and go for it.

SUCCESS IS ABOUT PEOPLE

True success, the kind that will make you happy and fulfilled, isn't about money, fame, or power. It's about people and relationships. Healthy relationships are truly the keys to happiness, good health, and success.

On your deathbed, will you wish you had made more money, worked harder, or accumulated more material possessions? That's doubtful. More likely, you'll be wishing you had spent more time with your spouse, children, family, and friends. Do some research. Ask a few older friends, individuals you find to be caring and wise, how their perspectives have changed over the years. Where are their priorities today compared with when they were your age? How might they live their lives differently if they could do it over again?

Have you ever asked yourself, "Why am I here?" or "What is the meaning of life? What is the meaning of *my* life?" Many high achievers never slow down long enough to consider questions like these. But grappling with these questions can help you shift your focus from achievement to relationships.

Try imagining your own funeral and writing your eulogy. Who will be there? Who won't be? Why and why not? What did your life mean? What did you stand for? What did you accomplish? What is the legacy that you left behind? Is it the legacy you want?

Your children are part of your legacy. How are you affecting them? What morals and values are they learning from you, consciously or unconsciously? Will they learn to value relationships, balance, and emotional health, or will they learn to value achievement above all else? It's up to you.

You Are Not Alone

You're not perfect, and you've got problems. Big deal—everyone has problems. Most people's problems are not *the problem*. Usually *the problem* is that they are afraid to admit and address their issues.

This insecurity or fear is very common. Have you ever thought, *What will they think of me if they find out that_____?* or *I can't let anyone see the real me.*

For example, you might have a hard time managing your anger, and instead of just accepting this, admitting it, and working on it, you avoid thinking about it, deny the truth, or defend how you are. How much simpler and easier life gets when you can just admit your weaknesses or problems. You save so much energy—energy that you can use to change instead of hide.

Everyone wants to be loved, accepted, respected, valued, and appreciated. The fear is that you won't be because of your shortcomings. You have that conditional love picture in your head. So you think, *I've got to hide it. I can't let anyone see.* And this puts you back in that damaging control mode, which makes those problems worse.

Consider counseling; you'll wind up better for it. Solve those problems instead of hiding them. It can be valuable to obtain help in figuring out what your issues are and how to do something about them. Life does get better when you stop hiding your problems. Yet the most intense, driven, and controlling people are often the ones who are hiding the most perceived inadequacy and the most fear. If you're one of them, just know that you're probably not more inadequate than most of the rest of us. You're just more scared. Isn't it time to let go of the fear and to approach life differently? You can do it.

IT'S YOUR LIFE

So, it's your life. What are you going to do? Only you can choose how you will respond. Maybe you know that something's missing in your marriage or relationships. Maybe you've had a failed relationship or two in the past and are starting to consider your own role in the events.

In terms of marriage, the options are simple: stay in an unhealthy marriage, get a divorce, or change yourself and find fulfillment in your relationship. You make decisions all the time—which of these options sounds best?

Ideally, both parties in the relationship want to make their marriage rewarding and both choose to put forth the effort necessary to accomplish this. Even if your spouse isn't interested, therapy can still help you. This is because *your* life and relationships will be better when *you* grow emotionally regardless of what your partner chooses to do.

Some people choose to stay in loveless marriages, and some get divorced. It would be simplistic to suggest that everyone can always make his or her married life work out happily ever after. Experts disagree on whether staying married or getting a divorce is better for your children. The major question is the nature of the home environment. Just how bad is it? What are the children learning from this home situation? Remember, the way you approach your marriage and the interactions you have with your partner teach your children about relationships, for better or worse.

So ask yourself, "Would I rather our children come from a broken family or live in a broken family?" Answering this is not easy for anyone, especially when your emotions are raging. A therapist may be able to help with this decision, too.

It's Never Too Late to Change

If you recognize yourself in the pages of this book, don't fret. It's never too late to change. Dr. Ferretti worked with a ninety-three-year-old client with a lifelong anger management problem, which he overcame through therapy. Old dogs can learn new tricks, especially when they're motivated and invested in making meaningful change. If change happened for this gentleman, it could happen for you, too.

Can you change? Will you change? Will you wait for a crisis, or more than one crisis? Can you change now, before the next avoidable crisis? Yes, you can.

Go for it! Create more time to spend in relationships with your friends and family. Redirect some of your energy from achievement to personal growth, and aim to achieve a healthy and balanced life.

> **"Trying" Is Lying**
>
> How often do we "try" to do things that don't get done? Too often for most of us. Sometimes we are just looking to excuse ourselves from the work it takes to actually make a change. Are we lying to ourselves? Remember in the movie Star Wars when Yoda asks Luke Skywalker to get the ship out of the swamp? Luke says, "I'll give it a try." Yoda replies, "No! Try not. Do or do not. There is no try." Yoda's right. Stop trying. Start doing.

Will it be painful? Probably. But remember, there's a lot in it for you, too. Life really is more satisfying and fuller when you are more connected with people and less concerned about material things. *Believe it.* Learn it. *Act on it. Win the Love Fight!*

THE BOTTOM LINE:

- Eventually, most people realize that healthy relationships are the key to happiness in life. Unfortunately, many recognize this only after they have destroyed one or more relationships already.
- Success and significance are not the same. Many people think only of significance after they have achieved success. Ask yourself the deeper questions early. What makes a meaningful life? What will be the significance of my life?
- You don't have to be like everyone else. You don't have to be like your mom or dad. You can choose your own priorities in life. Choose wisely. Get started.

Life
begins and ends
with relationships.

Authors' Invitation

We wrote this book to help you with your relationships. Marriage should probably be your most important interpersonal relationship, but there is another relationship that is of higher priority. Do you have a relationship with God? Here are several things that we believe about God and man: God has created people with a need to be in relationships with others and with him; unless you are in a right relationship with God, your human relationships will suffer. God loves you, and if you seek him, you will find this to be true. Perhaps you have never given much thought to God. Many people, Achievers and Connectors, haven't. We invite you to do so now. Let us know if we can help.

About the Authors

 DR. TONY FERRETTI is a licensed psychologist specializing in helping professionally successful clients with relationship problems. Dr. Ferretti holds bachelor's and master's degrees from the University of New York at Albany and received his PhD from the University of Southern Mississippi. For over twenty years, Dr. Ferretti has shared his expertise in psychology to help others recognize the addictive nature of power, control, and success. Dr. Ferretti has helped thousands of clients to achieve balance in their relationships and life.

An active blogger, sought-after public speaker, and seminar leader, Dr. Ferretti is a frequent media guest. He's appeared on the *Dr. Phil* show and hosted his own radio show, *Talk to Tony*, for nearly two years. Although a high achiever himself, Dr. Ferretti "walks the talk" by seeking balance in his life and keeping his priorities in a healthy order. Happily married for over twenty years with three children, he lives and practices in Central Florida. For more information, visit *DrTonyFerretti.com*

DR. PETER WEISS is a physician and health care executive with a passion for helping others to physical and emotional health. Dr. Weiss holds bachelor of arts and doctor of medicine degrees from Washington University in St. Louis. Formerly in the practice of Internal Medicine and Infectious Disease, he currently serves as an executive with the Adventist Health System located in Orlando, Florida.

Over his career from the bedside to the boardroom, Dr. Weiss has seen talented friends and colleagues lose their marriages through misplaced priorities. As a high-powered professional himself, he has changed his own priorities and tempered his interpersonal style in order to develop and sustain close relationships. Married for over twenty-five years, he lives with his wife, Sharon, in Orlando, Florida. For more information, visit *HealthDiscipleship.com*

FLORIDA HOSPITAL

The skill to heal. The spirit to care.®

Florida Hospital Celebration Health

Florida Hospital Altamonte

Florida Hospital Orlando

Florida Hospital Winter Park

Walt Disney Pavilion *at*
Florida Hospital for Children

Florida Hospital East Orlando

Florida Hospital Apopka

Florida Hospital Kissimmee

About the Publisher

For over one hundred years the mission of Florida Hospital has been: *To extend the health and healing ministry of Christ.* Opened in 1908, Florida Hospital is comprised of nine hospital campuses housing over 2,400 beds and twenty-two walk-in medical centers. With over 19,000 employees—including 2,200 doctors and 6,600 nurses— Florida Hospital serves the residents and guests of Orlando, the No. 1 tourist destination in the world. Florida Hospital has over 1.7 million patient visits a year. Florida Hospital is a Christian, faith-based hospital that believes in providing Whole Person Care to all patients – mind, body, and spirit. Hospital fast facts include:

+ **LARGEST ADMITTING HOSPITAL IN AMERICA**. Ranked No. 1 in the nation for inpatient admissions by the *American Hospital Association*.

+ **AMERICA'S HEART HOSPITAL**. Ranked No. 1 in the nation for number of heart procedures performed each year, averaging 22,000 cases annually. MSNBC named Florida Hospital "America's Heart Hospital" for being the No. 1 hospital fighting America's No. 1 killer—heart disease.

+ **HOSPITAL OF THE FUTURE**. At the turn of the century, the *Wall Street Journal* named Florida Hospital the "Hospital of the Future."

+ **ONE OF AMERICA'S BEST HOSPITALS**. Recognized by *U.S. News & World Report* as "One of America's Best Hospitals" for ten years. Clinical specialties recognized have included: Cardiology, Orthopaedics, Neurology & Neurosurgery, Urology, Gynecology, Digestive Disorders, Hormonal Disorders, Kidney Disease, Ear, Nose & Throat, and Endocrinology.

+ **LEADER IN SENIOR CARE**. Florida Hospital serves the largest number of seniors in America through Medicare with a goal for each patient to experience a "Century of Health" by living to a healthy hundred.

+ **TOP BIRTHING CENTER**. *Fit Pregnancy* magazine named Florida Hospital one of the "Top 10 Best Places in the Country to have a Baby." As a result, *The Discovery Health Channel* struck a three-year production deal with Florida Hospital to host a live broadcast called "Birth Day Live." Florida Hospital annually delivers over 10,000 babies.

+ **CORPORATE ALLIANCES**. Florida Hospital maintains corporate alliance relationships with a select group of Fortune 500 companies including Disney, Nike, Johnson & Johnson, Philips, AGFA, and Stryker.

+ **DISNEY PARTNERSHIP**. Florida Hospital is the Central Florida health & wellness resource of the *Walt Disney World*® Resort. Florida Hospital also partnered with Disney to build the ground breaking health and wellness facility called Florida Hospital Celebration Health located in Disney's town of Celebration, Florida. Disney and Florida Hospital recently partnered to build a new state-of-the-art Children's Hospital.

+ **HOSPITAL OF THE 21ST CENTURY**. Florida Hospital Celebration Health was awarded the *Premier Patient Services Innovator Award* as "The Model for Healthcare Delivery in the 21st Century."

+ **SPORTS EXPERTS**. Florida Hospital is the official hospital of the Orlando *Magic* NBA basketball team. In addition, Florida Hospital has an enduring track record of providing exclusive medical care to many sports organizations. These organizations have included: Disney's Wide World of Sports, Walt Disney World's Marathon Weekend, the Capital One Bowl, and University of Central Florida Athletics. Florida Hospital has also provided comprehensive healthcare services for the World Cup and Olympics.

+ **PRINT RECOGNITION**. *Self* magazine named Florida Hospital one of America's "Top 10 Hospitals for Women." *Modern Healthcare* magazine proclaimed it one of America's best hospitals for cardiac care.

+ **CONSUMER CHOICE AWARD WINNER**. Florida Hospital has received the Consumer Choice Award from the National Research Corporation every year from 1996 to the present.

Acknowledgments

People need help, especially people who write books. We'd like to acknowledge some of those who helped us with this one.

Dr. Tony Ferretti

Let me first acknowledge my counseling clients. Their courage inspires me as they share intimate details of their lives and engage in the difficult work of changing themselves to heal their relationships. Many of their stories have helped to shape this work.

Thank you to my wife, Allison, who is my greatest supporter. Her love means everything to me. Allison played an active editorial role in our writing, and the finished work is better for her efforts. Allison and our three daughters, Nicole, Valerie, and Danielle, were very patient during the long creative process. Their caring, support, and enthusiasm helped me more than they know.

My siblings Dan and Diann, along with my parents, cousins, and in-laws, shared insights and ideas along with much love and encouragement. The members of Trinity Presbyterian Church, especially those in my small group, have supported and prayed for me. Many other friends were similarly encouraging and steadfast in their confidence in me. Joyce Simpson has kept my clinical practice on schedule and running smoothly.

Dr. Peter Weiss, my co-author and friend, was consistently optimistic and hard working. I appreciate our partnership and his collaborative spirit.

Most importantly, I thank God for all of my blessings, including the help of the people above and the completion of this book.

DR. PETER WEISS

Let me acknowledge my wife, Sharon, from whom I have learned many valuable lessons. Thank you, Sharon, for all of your love and support over the years, and thank you for helping to make our marriage great.

I could not have found a better collaborator than my co-author, Dr. Tony Ferretti. Working with Tony allowed us both to live the values and model the behaviors we write about. Thank you, Tony.

Many friends have encouraged and continue to encourage me in all aspects of my life, including my writing. You know who you are. Thank you. Finally, I thank God for everything.

TONY FERRETTI AND DR. PETER WEISS

We would both like to acknowledge the many individuals who provided critical input into the manuscript as it was being written. Thank you Dr. Aliza Rosen, Stephanie Lind, Dr. Herdley Paolini, Dr. Karen Tilstra, Bethany Brown, Dr. Ted Hamilton, Dr. Theresa Schultz, Dr. Earnest Seiler, and Dr. Daniel Stump. A special thanks to Todd Chobotar and Dr. David Biebel of Florida Hospital Publishing. And we also thank Katie Cavinder, who helped with the research for this book.

Endnotes

Introduction

1   U.S. Department of Health and Human Services, "Births, Marriages, Divorces, and Deaths: Provisional Data for 2009," *National Vital Statistics Report* 58 (2010): 25.

2   Source: Jennifer Baker, Director of the Post-Graduate Program in Marriage and Family Therapy at Forest Institute of Professional Psychology in Springfield, MO, as reported on http://divorcestatistics.org.

3   D. Knox, U. Corte, "Work It Out/See A Counselor: Advice from Spouses in the Separation Process," *Journal of Divorce & Remarriage* 48 (2007): 1–2.

Chapter 2: They Don't Understand Me

1   "The Health Benefits of Strong Relationships, from Harvard Women's Health Watch." Posted online at: http://www.health.harvard.edu/press_releases/the-health-benefits-of-strong-relationships (accessed August 28, 2014).

2   "Social Relationships Are Key to Health, and to Health Policy," The PLoS Medicine Editors, Aug. 31, 2010. Posted online at: http://www.plosmedicine.org/article/info:doi/10.1371/journal.pmed.1000334 (accessed August 28, 2014).

Chapter 3: Better Together

1   P.R. Amato, D. Previti, "People's Reason for Divorcing: Gender, Social Class, The Life Course, and Adjustment," *Journal of Family Issues* 27 (2003): 602–606.

2   J.M. Gottman, L.J. Krokoff, "Marital Interaction and Satisfaction: A Longitudinal View," *Journal of Consulting and Clinical Psychology* 57 (1989): 47–52.

3   C.L. Cohan, T.N. Bradbury, "Negative Life Events, Marital Interaction, and the Longitudinal Course of Newlywed Marriage," *Journal of Personality and Social Psychology* 73 (1997): 114–128.

4   F.D. Fincham, S.R.H. Beach, J. Davila, "Longitudinal Relations Between Forgiveness and Conflict Resolution in Marriage," *Journal of Family Psychology* 18 (2004): 72–81.

5   M.E. McCullough, E.L. Worthington Jr., K.C. Rachal, "Interpersonal Forgiving in Close Relationships," *Journal of Personality and Social Psychology* 73 (1997): 321–336.

6   John Gray, *Men Are From Mars, Women Are From Venus* (New York: HarperCollins, 1992).

7   Gary Chapman, *The Five Love Languages* (Chicago: Northfield Publishing, 1995).

8   See: "The National Health and Social Life Survey" at: http://popcenter.uchicago.edu/data/nhsls.shtml.

9   Numerous articles support this claim, including: http://www.ianrpubs.unl.edu/pages/publicationD.jsp?publicationId=1510.

Chapter 4: Life Can Be a Battlefield

1   M.R. Nelson, S. Shavitt, "Horizontal and Vertical Individualism and Achievement Values: A Multi-Method Examination of Denmark and the United States," *Journal of Cross-Cultural Psychology* 33 (2002): 439–458.

2   S. Lyubomirsky, *The How of Happiness: A New Approach to Getting the Life You Want* (New York: The Penguin Press, 2008).

3   D. Myers, "The Funds, Friends and Faith of Happy People," *American Psychologist* 55 (2000): 56–67.

4   T. Kasser, *The High Price of Materialism* (Cambridge, MA: MIT Press, 2003).

5   T. Kasser, "Ecological Challenges, Materialistic Values, and Social Change," In R. Biswas-Diener (Ed.), *Positive Psychology as a Force of Social Change* (New York: Springer, 2011), 89–108.

6   "Non-Verbal Communication Modes." Posted online at: http://www.andrews.edu/~tidwell/bsad560/NonVerbal.html (accessed August 28, 2014).

7   H. Helms-Erikson, J.L. Tanner, A.C. Crouter, S. McHale, "Do Women's Provider Attitudes Moderate the Links Between Work and Family?" *Journal of Family Psychology* 14 (2000): 658–70.

8   S.D. Friedman, J.H. Greenhaus, *Work and Family—Allies or Enemies?: What Happens When Business Professionals Confront Life Choices* (New York: Oxford University Press, 2000).

9   David L. Altheide, "Mass Media, Crime, and The Discourse of Fear," The Hedgehog Review, 2003. Posted online at: http://www.iasc-culture.org/THR/archives/Fear/5.3CAltheide.pdf (accessed August 28, 2014).

10 Mary Kay Blakely, "A Snapshot Feature in USA Today," Columbia World of Quotations, Columbia University Press, 1996. Posted online at: http://quotes.dictionary.com/search/a_snapshot_feature (accessed August 28, 2014).

Chapter 5: Five Ways to a Power Failure

1   R. Helson, V.S.Y. Kwan, O.P. John, C. Jones, "The Growing Evidence for Personality Change in Adulthood: Findings from Research with Personality Inventories," *Journal of Research in Personality* 36 (2002): 287–306.

2   B.W. Roberts, K.E. Walton, W. Viechtbauer, "Patterns of Mean-Level Change in Personality Traits Across the Life Course: A Meta-Analysis of Longitudinal Studies," *Psychological Bulletin* 132 (2006): 1–25.

3   P.N. Lopes, M.A. Brackett, J.B. Nezlek, A. Schutz, I. Sellin, P. Salovey, "Emotional Intelligence and Social Interaction," *Personality and Social Psychology Bulletin* 30 (2004): 1018–1034.

4   N.S. Schutte, J.M. Malouff, C. Bobik, T. Conston, C. Greeson, C. Jedlicka, E. Rhodes, & G. Wendorf, "Emotional Intelligence and Interpersonal Relations," *Journal of Social Psychology* 141 (2001): 523–536.

5   D. Goleman, *Emotional Intelligence: Why It Can Matter More Than IQ* (New York: Bantam Books, 1995).

6   D.D. Burns, "The Perfectionist's Script for Self-Defeat," *Psychology Today* (November 1980): 34–52.

7   M. Haring, P.L. Hewitt, & G.L. Flett, "Perfectionism, Coping and Quality of Intimate Relationships," *Journal of Marriage and Family* 65 (2003): 143–158.

Chapter 6: What Are You Fighting For?

1   N.C. Overall, G.J.O. Fletcher, J.A. Simpson, & C.G. Sibley, "Regulating Partners in Intimate Relationships: The Costs and Benefits of Different Communication Strategies," *Journal of Personality and Social Psychology* 96 (2009): 620–639.

2   L.Y. Abramson, M.E.P. Seligman, J.D. Teasdale, "Learned Helplessness in Humans: Critique and Reformulation," *Journal of Abnormal Psychology* 87 (1978): 49–74.

3   M.P. Koss, "The Women's Mental Health Research Agenda: Violence Against Women," *American Psychologist* 45 (1990): 374–380.

4   "National Intimate Partner and Sexual Violence Survey-2010 Summary Report," CDC, 2010. Posted online at: http://www.cdc.gov/ViolencePrevention/pdf/NISVS_Report2010-a.pdf (accessed August 28, 2014.)

Chapter 7: History Is Not Destiny

1   J.S. Wallerstein, J.M. Lewis, "The Unexpected Legacy of Divorcing: Report of a 25-Year Study" *Psychoanalytic Psychology* 21 (2004): 353–370.

2   N.M. Melhem, M. Walker, G. Moritz, D. Brent, "Antecedent and Sequelae of Sudden Parental Death in Offspring and Surviving Caregivers," *Archives of Pediatrics and Adolescent Medicine* 162(2008): 403–410.

3   J.A. Andrews, S.L. Foster, D. Capaldi, H. Hops, "Adolescent and Family Predictors of Physical Agression, Communication, and Satisfaction in Young Adult Couples: A Prospective Analysis," *Journal of Consulting and Clinical Psychology* 68 (2000): 195–208.

4   Rosana E. Norman, Munkhtsetseg Byambaa, Rumna De, Alexander Butchart, James Scott, Theo Vos, "The Long-Term Health Consequences of Child Physical Abuse, Emotional Abuse, and Neglect: A Systematic Review and Meta-Analysis," *PLOS Medicine* 1001349 (2012): accessed August 28, 2014, DOI: 10.1371. Posted online at:
http://www.plosmedicine.org/article/info:doi/10.1371/journal.pmed.1001349.

5   Child Welfare Information Gateway, "Long-Term Consequences of Child Abuse and Neglect," 2013, US Department of Health and Human Services, Children's Bureau. Posted online at:
https://www.childwelfare.gov/pubs/factsheets/long_term_consequences.pdf (accessed August 28, 2014).

6   MerriamWebster.com defines sublimate as: "to divert the expression of (an instinctual desire or impulse) from its unacceptable form to one that is considered more socially or culturally acceptable."

7   J. Neal, D. Frick-Hornby, "The Effects of Parenting Styles and Childhood Attachment Patterns on Intimate Relationships," *Journal of Instructional Psychology* 28 (2001): 178–183.

Chapter 8: Finding Fame, Losing Love

1   J. Crocker, L.E. Park, "The Costly Pursuit of Self-Esteem," *Psychological Bulletin* 130 (2004): 392–414.

Chapter 9: Falling in Love Again

1   D.C. Atkins, R.A. Marin, T.T.Y. Lo, N. Klann, K. Hahlweg, "Outcomes of Couples with Infidelity in a Community-Based Sample of Couple Therapy," *Journal of Family Psychology* 24 (2010): 212–216.

2   "Mental Health: Does Therapy Work?" *Consumer Reports* (November 1995): 734–739.

3   B.E. Wampold, *The Great Psychotherapy Debate: Models, Methods and Findings* (London: Routledge, 2001).

4   "Attitudes to Counselling & Psychotherapy – Key Findings," June 2010, British Association for Counselling & Psychotherapy. Posted online at: http://www.itsgoodtotalk.org.uk/assets/docs/Attitudes-to-Counselling-Psychotherapy-Key-Findings-BACP-June-2010_1331121114.pdf (accessed August 28, 2014).

5   These steps are adapted from a variety of published resources and organized in a way that Dr. Ferretti has found most useful for couples needing guidance in this arena.

6   D.C. Atkins, K.A. Eldridge, D.H. Baucom, A. Christensen, "Infidelity and Behavioral Couple Therapy: Optimism in the Face of Betrayal," *Journal of Consulting and Clinical Psychology* 73 (2005): 144–150.

Chapter 12: Join the Fight!

1   D. Myers, "The Funds, Friends, and Faith of Happy People," *American Psychologist* 55 (2000): 56–67.

2   M. Tashman, K.R. Dougherty, *The Essential Guide to a Lasting Marriage* (New York: The Penguin Group, 2011).

3   L.J. Waite, M. Gallagher, *The Case for Marriage* (New York: Doubleday, 2000).

Notes

Notes

LEAD YOUR COMMUNITY
TO HEALTHY
LIVING

INCLUDES ONLINE TRAINING

Seminar Leader Kit
Everything a leader needs to conduct this seminar successfully, including key questions to facilitate group discussion and PowerPoint™ presentations for each of the eight principles.

Participant Guide
A study guide with essential information from each of the eight lessons along with outlines, self-assessments, and questions for people to fill in as they follow along.

Small Group Kit
It's easy to lead a small group using the CREATION Health videos, the Small Group Leader Guide, and the Small Group Discussion Guide.

CREATION Kids
CREATION Health Kids can make a big difference in homes, schools, and congregations. Lead kids in your community to healthier, happier living.

Life Guide Series
These guides include questions designed to help individuals or small groups study the depths of every principle and learn strategies for integrating them into everyday life.

GUIDES AND ASSESSMENTS

Pregnancy Guides
Expert advice on how to be CREATION Healthy while expecting.

Senior Guide
Share the CREATION Health principles with seniors and help them be healthier and happier as they live life to the fullest.

Self-Assessment
This instrument raises awareness about how CREATION Healthy a person is in each of the eight major areas of wellness.

Pocket Guide
A tool for keeping people committed to living all of the CREATION Health principles daily.

Tote Bag
A convenient way for bringing CREATION Health materials to and from class.

Tumbler
Practice good Nutrition and keep yourself hydrated with a CREATION Health tumbler in an assortment of fun colors.

MARKETING MATERIALS

Postcards, Posters, Stationery, and more
You can effectively advertise and generate community excitement about your CREATION Health seminar with a wide range of available marketing materials such as enticing postcards, flyers, posters, and more.

Bible Stories
God is interested in our physical, mental, and spiritual well-being. Throughout the Bible you can discover the eight principles for full life.

CREATION HEALTH BOOKS

CREATION Health Discovery
Written by Des Cummings Jr., PhD, Monica Reed, MD, and Todd Chobotar, this wonderful companion resource introduces people to the CREATION Health philosophy and lifestyle.

CREATION Health Devotional
In this devotional you will discover stories about experiencing God's grace in the tough times, God's delight in triumphant times, and God's presence in peaceful times.

English: Hardcover
Spanish: Softcover

CREATION Health Discovery (Softcover)

CREATION Health Discovery takes the 8 essential principles of CREATION Health and melds them together to form the blueprint for the health we yearn for and the life we are intended to live.

Pain Free For Life (Hardcover)

In *Pain Free For Life*, Scott C. Brady, MD,—founder of Florida Hospital's Brady Institute for Health—shares his dramatically successful solution for chronic back pain, fibromyalgia, chronic headaches, irritable bowel syndrome, and other "impossible to cure" pains. Dr. Brady leads pain-racked readers to a pain-free life using powerful mind-body-spirit strategies—where more than 80 percent of his chronic-pain patients have achieved 80–100 percent pain relief within weeks.

If Today Is All I Have (Softcover)

At its heart, Linda's captivating account chronicles the struggle to reconcile her three dreams of experiencing life as a "normal woman" with the tough realities of her medical condition. Her journey is punctuated with insights that are at times humorous, painful, provocative, and life-affirming.

SuperSized Kids (Hardcover)

In *SuperSized Kids*, Walt Larimore, MD, and Sherri Flynt, MPH, RD, LD, show how the mushrooming childhood obesity epidemic is destroying children's lives, draining family resources, and pushing America dangerously close to a total healthcare collapse—while also explaining, step by step, how parents can work to avert the coming crisis by taking control of the weight challenges facing every member of their family.

SuperFit Family Challenge – Leader's Guide

Perfect for your community, church, small group, or other settings.
The SuperFit Family Challenge Leader's Guide Includes:
- Eight weeks of pre-designed PowerPoint™ presentations.
- Professionally designed marketing materials and group handouts from direct mailers to reading guides.
- Training directly from Author Sherri Flynt, MPH, RD, LD, across six audio CDs.
- Media coverage and FAQ on DVD.

Forgive To Live (English: Hardcover / Spanish: Softcover)

In *Forgive to Live* Dr. Tibbits presents the scientifically proven steps for forgiveness—taken from the first clinical study of its kind conducted by Stanford University and Florida Hospital.

Forgive To Live Workbook (Softcover)

This interactive guide will show you how to forgive – insight by insight, step by step—in a workable plan that can effectively reduce your anger, improve your health, and put you in charge of your life again, no matter how deep your hurts.

Forgive To Live Devotional (Hardcover)

In his powerful new devotional, Dr. Dick Tibbits reveals the secret to forgiveness. This compassionate devotional is a stirring look at the true meaning of forgiveness. Each of the fifty-six spiritual insights includes motivational Scripture, an inspirational prayer, and two thought-provoking questions. The insights are designed to encourage your journey as you begin to *Forgive to Live*.

Forgive To Live God's Way, A Small Group Resource (Softcover)

Forgiveness is so important that our very lives depend on it. Churches teach us that we should forgive, but how do you actually learn to forgive? In this spiritual workbook, noted author, psychologist, and ordained minister Dr. Dick Tibbits takes you step-by-step through an eight-week forgiveness format that is easy to understand and follow.

Forgive To Live Leader's Guide

Perfect for your community, church, small group, or other settings.
The Forgive To Live Leader's Guide Includes:

- Eight weeks of pre-designed PowerPoint™ presentations.
- Professionally designed customizable marketing materials and group handouts on CD-Rom.
- Training directly from author of *Forgive to Live* Dr. Dick Tibbits across six audio CDs.
- Media coverage DVD.
- CD-Rom containing all files in digital format for easy home or professional printing.
- A copy of the first study of its kind conducted by Stanford University and Florida Hospital showing a link between decreased blood pressure and forgiveness.

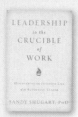

Leadership in the Crucible of Work (Hardcover)

What is the first and most important work of a leader? (The answer may surprise you.) In *Leadership in the Crucible of Work*, noted speaker, poet, and college president Dr. Sandy Shugart takes readers on an unforgettable journey to the heart of what it means to become an authentic leader.

CREATION Health Breakthrough (Hardcover)

Blending science and lifestyle recommendations, Monica Reed, MD, prescribes eight essentials that will help reverse harmful health habits and prevent disease. Discover how intentional choices, rest, environment, activity, trust, relationships, outlook, and nutrition can put a person on the road to wellness. Features a three-day total body rejuvenation therapy and four-phase life transformation plan.

CREATION Health Devotional for Women (English)

Written for women by women, the *CREATION Health Devotional for Women* is based on the principles of whole-person wellness represented in CREATION Health. Spirits will be lifted and lives rejuvenated by the message of each unique chapter. This book is ideal for women's prayer groups, to give as a gift, or just to buy for your own edification and encouragement.

A Desk Reference to Personalizing Patient Care (Hardcover)

Aurora Realin, MBA, CDM, discusses how diversity is increasing at a rapid pace. Clinicians committed to providing the best patient care must become familiar with the key attitudes and expectations of patients whose culture, religious beliefs, generation, or level of disability differs from their own.

Now there is help. *Personalizing Patient Care* is a valuable guide for improving a caregiver's understanding of how a patient's background may affect their needs, preferences, and expectations related to the delivery of care.

HEAR MORE FROM DR. PETER WEISS

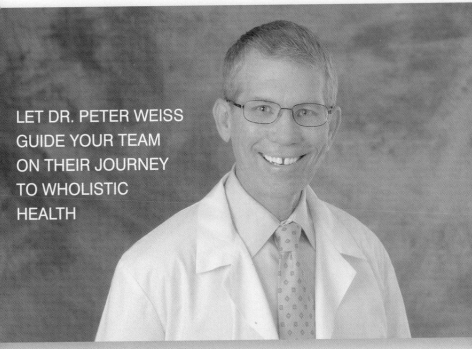

LET DR. PETER WEISS
GUIDE YOUR TEAM
ON THEIR JOURNEY
TO WHOLISTIC
HEALTH

DR. WEISS SPEAKS ON MANY TOPICS INCLUDING:

+ **The Love Fight**
  How Achievers and Connectors Can Build a Marriage That Lasts

+ **Better Together**
  Discovering the Essentials of a Strong Marriage

+ **More Health, Less Care**
  Creating a Healthy Lifestyle

+ **Write Your Personal Prescription**
  Being Your Own Advocate in Healthcare

+ **Willpower Is Not the Answer**
  Thinking Differently About the Connection Between Physical,
  Emotional, and Spiritual Health

To book Dr. Weiss or another speaker for your event, visit
www.FloridaHospitalPublishing.com

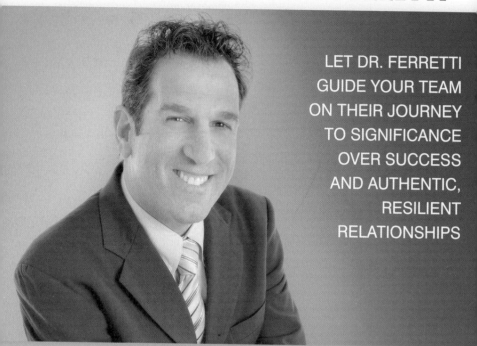